Growing Succulents

A Pictorial Guide

Shoichi Tanabe

TUTTLE Publishing

Tokyo | Rutland, Vermont | Singapore

Contents

How to Use This Book

Part 1 "Enjoying Plant Arrangements" introduces plant arrangement and presents a few examples.
Part 2 "Basics of Cultivation" introduces the basics of growing plants including the choice of soil and fertilizers, watering, and temperature control. I recommend to people not yet used to growing succulent plants to be sure to read Part 2 of this book.
Part 3 "Illustrations of most popular succulents" introduces 712 different species in total. The order is mostly alphabetical based on their scientific name (Latin name following the APG classification system), but there are slight modifications in the order as well.
–If there are terms you're not familiar with, please refer to the glossary on p.166–169.

Ease of Growth
★★★ Easy / ★★☆ Normal / ★☆☆ Difficult

Country of origin
The main region the plant is originally from

Species-specific tips and characteristics
displays useful info

Alternative names
A summary of alternative names

Petit Care
Displays tips on how to replant, take care or grow the plants, with detailed photos included

Characteristics
Features the common points of that family

Scientific name
Please refer to p.168 for the list of scientific names

Family name
Genus name

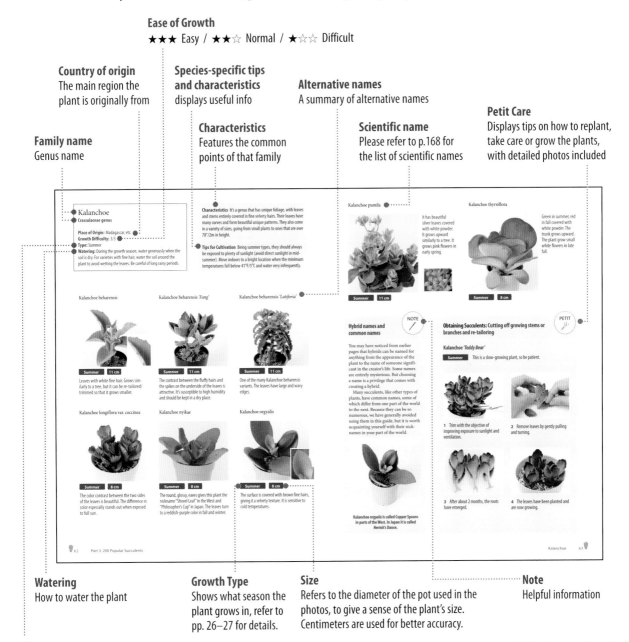

Watering
How to water the plant

Growth Type
Shows what season the plant grows in, refer to pp. 26–27 for details.

Size
Refers to the diameter of the pot used in the photos, to give a sense of the plant's size. Centimeters are used for better accuracy.

Note
Helpful information

Type
Shows whether the genus is summer type, winter type or spring-fall type.

This manual is based on growing succulents in the Eastern region of Japan, which ranges from zone 3a tp zone 13a. Take this in account when growing plants in areas with different temperatures.

Why I Wrote This Book

Lately, many people have started to grow and enjoy succulent plants.

I often hear people say it's their first time growing succulents, or they have lots of questions for me whenever they come to my shop. As someone who's been loving succulents and cacti since I was a kid, all of this makes me very happy.

On the other hand, I also often hear of people giving up on succulents because they think they're too hard to grow and care for. I believe the reason these people's succulents don't grow well is simply that they have been trying to grow them similarly to other common plants, or perhaps they have been trying to grow them exclusively indoors.

Succulents are charming plants with their stems, leaves and roots full of nutrients and water. Succulents generally grow in arid regions where the soil has few nutrients and temperature differences can be very drastic.

When growing succulents, you have to consider the ways of the seasons in your growing area. For example, in Japan, summers are hot and humid, with about six very rainy weeks that vary in timing depending on location. Fall too has long rainy periods, and winters are very cold. Also keep in mind that succulents' need differs from those of other plants; they are not, however, very difficult to care for by any means.

Imagine what it would be like if you lived your entire life in an arid region and suddenly moved to a humid, subtropical climate, or from a hot southern region to a cool northern one. The change in humidity and coldness of winter could make you susceptible to illness. The same is true of plants: try to imagine what kind of environment your succulent plants would comfortably grow in and take care of them accordingly.

This book provides some of the basic rules for growing succulent plants, such as watering, how to deal with extreme temperatures, growth calendars for each species, daily maintenance rules and other tips for growing succulents. The illustrated part also includes a large variety of species, from easy-to-grow to very difficult to grow ones.

You may fail at first, but there's plenty to learn from mistakes, and it's good to think of them as a necessary step in the learning process. For example, if you water your plants too much, the roots will rot and wither; or if you leave your plant outside during the winter too without knowing it's a summer plant, it may wither from the cold.

In failure lies the key to having a long and fruitful relationship with your succulent plants. Whenever you make a mistake, consider what may have gone wrong and use your acquired knowledge to your advantage the next time you try. Repeating this process, you will slowly find yourself getting better and better at growing succulents.

I put together and summarized everything I teach to customers who visit my shop in this single book. I hope this book will help you enjoy a wonderful life with succulent plants.

—**Shoichi Tanabe** (from Tanabe Flower)

1

Plant Arrangements

The shape, overall form and color of succulents can be very diverse. Succulents can be arranged both by themselves and in a mixed arrangement of various species. When arranging multiple species, you can enjoy glorious diversity in a single pot. The key to a successful arrangement is to combine species that need to be cared for in the same way.

Arrangements with Drought-resistant Plants

Arrangements consisting only of succulents are very common, but in this case I tried arranging succulents with plants that can resist droughts. Plants that are native to Australia, New Zealand, South Africa and the Mediterranean region are often tolerant to long periods without water. The key is to choose some plants that share your succulents' watering and temperature needs.

Existing arrangements can guide you, but before you look at them, try designing an arrangement on your own, so you won't limit your own imagination with preconceived ideas.

This impressive plant with bronze-colored branches is called Corokia cotoneaster. It's native to New Zealand and while it has a strong resistance to cold, it's weak to humid heat; preferring a dry environment, similar to succulents. I tried arranging Corokia with Sedum. The plant in the foreground is a Creeping Thyme. Other dryness-resistant herbs like Rosemary can also be used.

Note how the color of the pot harmon-izes with the color of the flowering Sedums.

? **Nice herbal accents with interesting branching and simple sedum**

Mixed Arrangements

2

’ **Arranging plants with beautiful and expressive foliage: Lithops and Pleiospilos**

It is believed that Lithops and Pleiospilos have evolved to mimic stones to protect themselves from harm.

This arrangement combines them with Lotus brimstone, native to the Mediterranean Sea, with white stones also arranged casually around them. Brimstone likes dry areas and can grow in low temperatures too.

The Crassula in the center and the drooping Senecio on the left give a sense of movement to the arrangement.

Mixed Arrangements

3

’ **An elegant arrangement of colored succulents, with a light and beautiful feel.**

In this arrangement I chose nicely colored succulents to match the color of the pot. It's an arrangement with bold movement in mind, implementing Gossiper, Sedum, Graptopetalum, Senecio and some other species.

" Tonal colors creating a graceful atmosphere in a tall terracotta pot.

I planted Echeveria and Pachyphytum in the center and arranged Grevillea's crawling branches around the pot. Then I added some drooping Senecio in the front to give a more nuanced accent to the arrangement.

" A beautiful scene to enjoy red foliage full of life in the winter.

Succulent arrangements slowly grow with time and tend to twist and turn freely. The Aloe in the back and the Echeveria arranged around the center protect the sedum in the middle. If you keep the arrangement healthy for about ten years, it grows strong enough to be left outside all year round.

Mixed Arrangements

6

9 **A bold arrangement of large and small caudices**

Caudex varieties are often grown as a single plant, but as long as you grow multiple plants in the same pot and you take care of them in the same way, they can be grown together too. However, keep in mind that caudices are very sensitive to repotting, so absolutely avoid repotting in winter. It is possible to replant in May or June, however.

In the picture, Pachypodium cactiensis in the back, Pachypodium rothratum is on the left and Pachypodium brevicauleis on the right.

Mixed Arrangements

7

9 **A cohesive arrangement with colorful reds in an equally colorful pot.**

The color of the plant matches the color of the pot to create a cohesive arrangement. The Aeonium adds height to the arrangement and balances nicely with the plants in the front. Without planting the succulents too close to each other, I arranged them with some red sand. The succulents are also arranged in different directions so they look nice from all angles.

A Gathering of Succulents Only

The Echeveria is the star of the show in its large pot. When creating large arrangements, the key is to have a leading plant and correctly choose where to place the "gravitational point." Choose as your lead a large and colorful plant that catches the eye, and let's create a nice, balanced arrangement by placing the lead just slightly off the center of the gravitational point of the arrangement.

In this case, I chose to plant Echeveria and Sedum in a dynamic arrangement.

Mixed
Arrangements

8

With Echeveria in the dominant role, enjoy creating a large arrangement.

Add other succulents to your grouping. A "succulents only" combination is a mainstay of succulent gardening. The key to healthy grouping is combining plants of the same "growth type." Be mindful of the shape of each stock and plant them in a three-dimensional form. A small-container combination makes a charming arrangement. A large-container combination makes a dynamic one. Consider your arrangement carefully. With a large arrangement, you want to determine the "main characters" and the center of gravity. When colorful, eye-catching plants play the starring roles, place the center of gravity on the left and aim for balance and a sense of firmness in your arrangement. Here, I went for a dynamic arrangement with Echeveria and Sedum balancing each other.

, A gorgeous and brilliant arrangement

In this arrangement, I chose plants similar in size and growth schedules (optimal seasons) and planted them closely to each other, such as Sedum and Echeveria. The arrangement has a very cute and "classic succulent" feel to it.

, Using height variation to give movement

Placing taller plants in the back and shorter ones a bit closer, and drooping branches around is the basic pattern.

I recommend avoiding placing drooping branches in the front and placing them on the sides instead to create more movement.

Steps and Tips for Arrangements

It is important to imagine what the arrangement will look like once it grows or after replanting, while keeping in mind the balance of colors and the size differences among your plants. So choose the plants you want to use based on those considerations.

Let's then move onto the steps for arranging your plants.

Main steps:

Tips

1. Select a variety of plants that require similar management.
Because we are planting multiple species in the same pot, check the optimal season (winter-type, summer type etc.), and choose plants with similar management requirements (such as watering or placement) among those in the same type.

2. Choose the positioning of your plants depending on the angle you want view the arrangement from.
If the viewing angle is from the front, I recommend placing taller plants in the back and shorter plants in the front. If the viewing angle is from above, pay attention to the color and shape of the plants.

3. Should I choose the pot or the arrangement first?
The combination of arrangement and pot is also important. Do you choose a pot you like first? Or do you start by choosing the plants you'd like to arrange? There's no one right answer here, but I base my choice on how I perceive the leading role.

4. Having a good balance of color and sizes.
It's difficult to achieve a balanced arrangement if you use too many plants of different sizes. Start by choosing the main subject of your arrangement and then consider the size of the other plants. You can choose to have either a colorful arrangement or a collection of similar colors.

What to Prepare:

A. Pumice stones (for the bottom of the pot)

B. Planting soil

C. Spray mist (spray bottle)

D. Planting pot (If it's difficult to differentiate front and back of the pot, mark one side with tape or something similar.)

E. Seedlings: 5 species from Echeveria, Sedum and Crassula

F. Netting for the bottom (Prevents pests from entering from the bottom and soil from falling off.)

G. Scissors (Sterilize with alcohol before using them.)

H. Plastic spoon

I. Tweezers (Sterilize with alcohol before using them.)

J. Dirt bags

Procedure:

1 Add the netting to the bowl.

2 Add the pumice stone in the bottom.

3 Fill the pot with planting soil until about half full.

4 Prepare the seedlings: start by loosening the roots.

15

5 Remove the lower leaves to make the seedling easier to plant. Also remove any dead leaves.

6 Cut roots that are too long.

7 The seedlings are ready to be planted.

8 Place the seedlings temporarily in the pot and try to imagine the final arrangement.

9 For right-handed people, it's easier to plant from left to right.

10 Add soil for each seedling you plant, turn the pot slightly as you plant them.

11 Gently thrust tweezers in the soil after each planting and push the roots in the soil.

12 By pushing the roots in like this, the direction of roots will hardly change, but the seedlings will grow loosely and close to each other, which makes their growth enjoyable to watch.

13 Fill the soil leaving no space. Use tweezers to thrust in the soil and push the roots in the spaces.

14 Adjust the placing of each seedling so their "face" is nice and visible. Also make sure they can get plenty of sunlight.

15 The last steps can be a bit difficult with dry soil, so wet the soil with a small amount of water.

16 Finally, add in any drooping plants and other plants, making sure to push their roots in the soil with tweezers.

Done!

17 Varieties with thin roots can be easily planted by pinching the roots with tweezers and pushing them into the soil.

18 Fill the gaps and the background with plants too.

Tip Wait one week before starting to water!

2

Cultivation Basics

The regions where succulents are native often have extreme temperature differences between day and night and rain is very rare, so most of these plants are resilient to arid lands; on the other hand, many regions have quite the opposite climate. The plump and thick roots you see here are proof of how succulents have adapted and matured in those non-native environments.

Succulents are naturally strong and resilient, but it's important to learn the basics of growing them in different climates from their native habitat.

Choosing Seedlings

The first step in cultivating succulents is choosing the right seedling. When you settle on an appealing variety (keeping your budget in mind), look for a seedling that's healthy and vigorous.

(Check if) Leaves and stems have nice and glossy color.

(Check if) The plant is free of disease and pests (more on p. 37).

(Check if) The stalks aren't growing erratically (not growing too long).

Checklist for choosing a seedling
Once you've decided on a variety among your available options, keeping the checklist at left in mind, look for a plant that looks healthy and is already growing nicely. This is key to cultivation success. It is also important to know the exact genus and variety of the plant you are buying. If the plant isn't labeled, ask the store staff for this important information. Note: many plants that aren't available to you locally may be obtainable online. Your chances of getting a plant that looks as good as the online photo are better if you check that the vendor is reputable, includes good information, is easy to contact, and responds to questions and posts.

Shop

Choosing a store
Specialty shops and garden stores are your safest bet!
Succulent specialty shops and gardening shops are the best places to buy succulents. This is because the succulents there are often kept in an optimal environment (p.20) with good lighting and ventilation. However, you might also encounter the plants you're looking for in other shops. Many home goods stores, superstores and warehouse clubs are selling succulents these days, and the plants themselves look healthy. If you happen to pass by a nice succulent you'd like to cultivate, it's okay to buy it. However, keep in mind that if it has been kept indoors for long, it may get burned from direct sunlight so make sure to get them used to sunlight gradually.

Season

Starting from spring is recommended.
If you are growing succulents for the first time, I recommend starting in spring or early summer. Most succulents are spring and fall-types (growing in spring and fall). When kept in a compatible climate during spring, they will grow well and healthily. By starting in spring, you will also grow accustomed to most of the basic challenges of cultivating succulents, such as dealing with humid weather in the rainy season and with the high temperatures and direct sunlight in summer. Also in spring, there are many varieties available in stores and the plants are often healthy. Spring to early summer is also the ideal time to buy summer-type succulents. This having been said, you can of course start whenever you'd like to start.

Price

Are cheap plants easy to grow?
Succulent prices can range from just a couple of dollars to hundreds. The main factor in price is the ease of growing and propagating. The species that are easier to grow and easily produce plenty of seeds can reproduce quickly and are less expensive, as they can be produced in large quantities. Therefore, we can say that most cheap varieties are easy to grow. Plants that are harder to grow in large quantities will naturally be more expensive, and plants that have been imported directly from their native regions are often very pricey. Because the climate is completely different when growing them outside of their native environments, they require experience and knowledge in cultivation.

How to grow successful succulents as a beginner

Even if you start out prepared and determined to grow nice succulents, success can be hard to achieve at first. But taking the first step is the only way to get anywhere. Trial and error gain you experience. These tips will help you take that first step.

Tips

1. Choose varieties that are easy to grow.
For beginners, Echeveria, Sedum or Agave are examples of good starter plants. They are inexpensive and tend to be hardy.

2. Check the growth type of your plant.
Always know in advance what genus and variety you're planting and check their growth type. Avoid plants about which you know nothing.

3. Get plenty of information from specialty stores.
I recommend buying your first plant from a succulent specialty store. It's good to ask a professional how to grow the variety you're choosing.

4. When replanting, move the original soil along too.
When replanting, don't remove the original soil from the roots; instead, replant in a slightly larger pot than the original and add more soil.

5. When arranging, only plant varieties of the same growth-type together.
If you want to arrange multiple plants in a single pot, it's best to arrange only plants of the same growth-type together, as it's difficult to grow multiple plants with different care requirements and growth periods in the same pot.

Five points for growing the popular caudex

Caudices (caudiciforms) are a plump plant variety with stems and roots that grow wild in arid and harsh environments. They are full of water and nutrients. Here are some tips for growing them in cooler, more humid environments.

Tips

1. Let the plant grow slowly.
If you want to grow plump, large plants, avoid using fertilizer as much as possible. Their growth will be slow, but in their native regions, they take 10–20 years to grow. All plants are wonderful to behold as they grow, so enjoy these plants' gradual unfolding.

2. Be careful to not overwater.
For summer-type plants, wait until the soil in the pot is completely dry before watering thoroughly. You can check the soil's dryness with a bamboo skewer/stick to make sure you're not overwatering.

3. Water just lightly once a month during its dormant season (not summer).
A a rule, when the plant drops leaves during the dormant season, water very sparingly. It's a tricky time, as very little water is optimal, but none at all can kill the plant. I recommend watering at least once a month during its dormant seasons, just lightly enough to get the surface of the soil wet.

4. Repot in early summer.
Caudex varieties are sensitive to replanting so leave 2–3 years between replantings. When you want to replant, it's recommended to do so in early summer, around May and June.

5. Seedlings are easy to grow.
For beginners, caudex plants grown in your general region are easier to care for than those imported from their native land.

Example of a plant grown here in Japan from seeds

Imported plant

Basics of Placement

Succulent plants should be placed outdoors rather than indoors. To grow healthy, they need sunshine and good ventilation.

Outdoors, Sunlight and Ventilation

Succulents have a very charming and unique appearance so I understand why people like to use them in interior decor. However, succulents are very different from so-called houseplants and they need plenty of sunlight. When kept indoors the sunlight won't even be close to be enough.

The three main principles of growing healthy succulents are *outdoors*, *sunlight* and *ventilation*. Keep that in mind every time you choose the placement for a succulent.

Not Enough Indoor Sunlight or Ventilation

Indoor sunlight and ventilation are just not enough for succulents.

As an example, in a sunny summer day, direct sunlight measures at around 100 thousand lux. Even on overcast days, it would be around 30 thousand lux (taking into account the values at noon).

Indoors however, even when measuring the light in front of a very bright and south-facing window, the light barely reaches around 8–9 thousand lux—about only a tenth of the maximum and a third of the minimum light available outdoors!

Indoor ventilation also isn't enough. When placing the pots indoors during winter, turn on a fan to blow air on your plants after watering.

A place where the rain doesn't reach
Roofs and eaves provide shelter from the rain and from strong direct sunlight in summer, protecting the plant.

Sunlight is essential
Make sure to place the pot in such a way that sunshine reaches your plants at a good angle. To protect weaker varieties from strong direct sunlight, you can use shade netting as a countermeasure. (p. 21)

Place on a stand or a rack
This helps with ventilation and temperature control. The balcony floor is poorly ventilated and the heat or cold would be directly transferred to the pot, so place the pots on stands or racks. Generally, it's good to have at least 4"/10cm between shelf and floor. However, when you have multiple pots in the same rack, be careful that the water from watering one pot doesn't reach other pots.

During the very humid season, artificially add wind
During summer or the rainy season, use a fan or similar to send a breeze to your plants and drive away moisture

Cultivation lights
If you want to grow your succulents indoors, cultivation lights come in handy. You can ask at specialty and gardening stores which varieties are more apt to grow with indoor lights and also ask what type of lamp is suitable for your space, temperature control and such.

Countermeasures for Sunlight, Humidity and Extreme Temperatures

In many of the native regions of succulents, days are hot but nights are cooler, with the air being a bit dry. Following are some tips for growing plants in Japan's hot and humid climate.

What is the climate in their native regions?

Succulents mostly originate from tropical area such as South Africa and Madagascar or Central and South America. Succulents are known for being very resilient in those tropical regions, with their strong sunlight and high temperatures. Keep in mind that most of their native habitats are found at higher altitudes, where temperatures usually reach up to 86°F/30°C during the day and drop down to around 64°F/18°C, and where the air is dry.

Succulents hate the summer in many regions

Most succulent plants have trouble surviving high temperatures, humidity, and strong sunlight. Strong sunlight often causes leaf burn, and at times can even cause the plant to wither.

It's not rare for the temperatures to be higher than 95°F/35°C during summer in some parts of the world, with a some days even exceeding 104°F/40°C, or even higher. In addition to that, summers in such regions can be very humid or rainy. When taking care of succulents, summer countermeasures are often more important than winter ones.

Protection against summer sun

Protect leaves from leaf burns

Succulents are full of water in their leaves and stems, because of this, unlike other plants, being exposed to strong sunlight may cause leaf burn (p. 37). Succulent leaves are very akin to human skin in that regard.

When growing succulents, it is very important that they get plenty of sunlight but to avoid leaf burn during summer, it is good to have some shading.

Basic shading and growth rules

For creating shade, shading nets are convenient and easy to set up, but they have the tendency to shade the plants too much. So I recommend a shading net with a shading rate of 50% for the best results with succulent plants (you can find shading nets of various rates in gardening stores or on the internet).

If you have shaded spaces, where sunlight only hits a few hours a day, shading may not be necessary in seasons other than midsummer.

*When "half shade" is mentioned later in the book, it means that the plant requires sunlight protection as explained above.

Summer Type Plants
Shading is not necessary, but it is recommended to use a fan(or similar method) to provide some breeze, in order to avoid the insides of the pot becoming too hot or humid.

Spring-Fall and Winter Type Plants
It's recommended to use shading nets to avoid strong sunlight. To avoid the insides of the pot becoming too hot or humid, occasionally use a fan (or similar method) to provide wind.

Protection against Rain and Humidity

Regulate watering during the rainy season or long rains.

For succulent plants, water generously at once, and then wait until the pot is fully dry on the inside before watering again. It is important to maintain a good balance between watering and drying. During the rainy season, or during long rains, even if the pots are protected by roofs, they will likely require more time to fully dry out. During these seasons, it is important to regulate how often you water the pots. If you usually water the pot once a week, you can for example water it only once every two weeks instead.

Protection against winter's cold weather

The key temperatures to remember are 41°F/5°C and 34°F/1°C.

Keep an eye on the daily minimum temperature to know when it's appropriate to take measures against the cold. I recommended to start taking measures once the minimum temperature drops under 41°F/ 41°F/5°C.

Before the minimum temperature drops below 41°F/ 41°F/5°C, move summer type plants indoors, in front of a bright window. For spring-fall and winter plants, they should be placed outdoors in full sunlight as long as the minimum temperature is above 43°F/ 6°C. When moving them indoors, do not place them in a warm room immediately, as sudden temperature changes aren't good for succulent plants.

Summer types should be moved indoors, in an area with little influence from the heating.

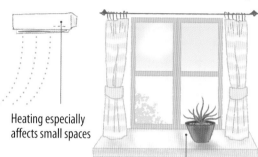

Heating especially affects small spaces

Occasionally use a fan on the plants and place them in front of bright windows.

Using non-woven (felt and such) fabric against cold

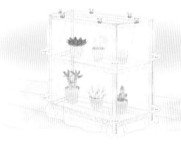

Spring-Fall and winter plants can be kept outside at temperatures as low as 34°F/ 1°C, but you can cover them with non-woven fabrics at night.

In case you're using a (simple/portable) greenhouse (vinyl or such)

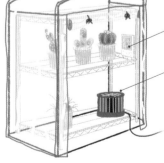

Be aware of high temperatures that may occur even during winter days if there's not enough ventilation.

Installation of thermometers and hygrometers.

Using a horticultural heater is recommended.

Temperature guidelines

Summer Types
Day 68°F/ 20°C Night 43°F/ 6°C

Spring- Fall, Winter Types
Day 50°F/10°C Night 34°F/ 1°C

Separate summer type plants and winter/spring-fall type plants into different greenhouses.

Summer Types
Watering
Water while there are still leaves on the plant. Once the leaves start falling, gradually reduce the frequency and the amount of water you give. When their leaves have fallen completely, stop watering altogether and let the plant go dormant.

Note for when to stop watering
You should stop watering thick- rooted species, however thin-rooted species will grow weak if left without any water whatsoever, so water just enough to dampen the soil's surface once a month.

Move indoors during winter
Before the minimum temperature drops below 41°F/ 41°F/5°C, move the plants indoors in front of a bright window. However, avoid heating the room too much.

Spring-Fall and Winter Types
Check Their Hardiness Zones
Some succulents, such as some types of Sedum and Sempervium, for example, can tolerate extreme cold. Check the hardiness zone of your plant as well your weather forecast.

Temperature Control
When in doubt, if he minimum temperature drops below 41°F/ 41°F/5°C or if snow is forecast, move the plants indoors in front of a bright window. Avoid heating the room too much.

Watering
Adjust the frequency and amount of water you give according to their growth type and species/variety.

Basics of Watering

Basics of appropriate watering.

There are two basic principles for watering succulent plants. The first one is to wait until the soil inside the pot is fully dry before watering, then water the pot enough that water runs out from the bottom of the soil. The second is to water gently so that the water doesn't drip on the leaves. Since their bodies are full of water, succulent plants are very sensitive to high humidity.

1. Watering should be the first thing you do when you wake up (first thing in the morning).

A basic rule of watering is doing it early in the morning. If you water the plants in the middle of the day, the water may warm up in the pot. This is extremely bad for the plants, especially in summer. Also, if you water during the morning, the water will evaporate by evening. However, if you water during the evening, it's unlikely that the water will evaporate by morning. It is very important for succulent plants to fully dry out after watering.

2. When the soil dries up, water generously.

It is difficult to tell how dry the soil is when you look at it from outside. A simple way to get around this problem is keeping a bamboo skewer (or similar) in the pot's soil. You can then pull the skewer out occasionally and check how wet the soil is. Alternatively, you can hold the pot before and after watering and feel the difference in weight, so that next time you can estimate how dry the soil is. As a basic of rule, you want to add enough water that it starts flowing from the bottom of the pot. Doing this helps to flush away waste and air out of the pot.

Check the appearance of the leaves.

Watering should be done according to the basic rules, but don't forget to check the appearance of the plant's leaves. If they become soft or discolored, it's likely you have watered the plant too much. If the leaves are whitish or faded, it's a sign of water deficiency. When the leaves are falling, the plant will enter its dormant period so reducing the amount and frequency of watering is important. Always keep an eye on the messages your plant is giving you.

How to water

Use a watering can with a narrow spout

Generally, you want to water the soil around the plant. Cheap cans are perfectly fine.

Shower watering

Water from above occasionally to get rid of dust or pests.

Watering the bottom

For small plants, or when leaves make it difficult to water the soil around, you can instead let water be absorbed from the bottom of the pot, the water will naturally flow upward. Stop watering immediately once the surface becomes damp.

Blower

Water droplets left on the leaves can cause leaf burn by accumulating sunlight. Use a blower to blow them away.

Insert a bamboo skewer in the soil.

Take it out to check the soil's moisture.

Don't do this.

Using a sprayer for watering doesn't let the water reach the roots. It only raises the humidity around the plant which is very bad.

Soil and Fertilizer

Commercial soil for growing succulents is fine, but you can also make your own soil.

Solid fertilizers are convenient as they dissolve little by little when watering.

Succulent-specific soil is widely available on the market. It has good drainage and water retention properties, pH (weak acidic) and it already has an adjusted amount of fertilizer blended in.

If you're not sure about what soil to get, check out the "recommended blend" section below.

Once you get used to growing succulents, you can blend the soil yourself. For example, you can try changing the mixture to suit your environment. Trying various mixtures and methods is one of the joys of cultivation, after all.

It is also important to replant regularly when dealing with succulent plants.

Try a change of soil after dividing and tailoring the roots.

Main soils used for cultivation

Seedling soil
When planting seedlings or leaf cuts, the roots are still thin and weak, so it's best to plant in specific soil for seedlings (with finer particles).

Akadama Soil (Small grains)
It is a weak acid soil made from red volcanic ash. Its properties and uses vary depending on grain size. Small grains have good water retention and drainage properties, while giving very good plant stability.

Pumice Stone
This porous stone gives excellent air permeability for the plants and the soil has good drainage and water retention properties. The color and properties of the soil vary slightly depending on the place of origin. In general however, Pumice stones are white or gray.

Kanuma Soil
This is a special type of pumice stone collected in the Kanuma region in Tochigi, Japan. It is lighter in weight and color than akadama soil. It is also very acidic and has excellent water retention and drainage properties.

Pearlite
Pearlite is a material that has been expanded via exposure to high temperatures; it is used as a soil supplement. Its characteristics are very similar to Vermiculite. In general, choose Vermiculite for water retention and Pearlite for water drainage.

Zeolite
A mineral formed from volcanic ash accumulated at the bottom of oceans or lakes, thanks to high water pressure and other factors. It is porous with micro-level holes, giving it top-class fertilizer retention and air permeability. It is used as a supplement to your main soil.

Vermiculite
Vermiculite exposed to high temperatures becomes a very good supplement to the main soil. It is porous and produces a soil with high water retention and drainage properties, while also having high fertilizer retention properties.

About Fertilizers
Succulents are plants that have adapted to survive in harsh environments. It is absolutely okay to use much less fertilizer than you would usually use for other flowers and plants. There are multiple types of fertilizers, but solid fertilizers that slowly release or granular chemical fertilizers are recommended.

Also, you shouldn't use fertilizers year-round: choose when to add fertilizers depending on the plant you're cultivating.
*see pp. 26–27 "Management Calendar"

Recommended Blend

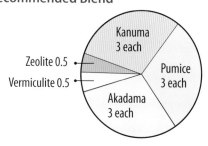

Zeolite 0.5 · Vermiculite 0.5 · Kanuma 3 each · Pumice 3 each · Akadama 3 each

Solid slow-releasing fertilizers (left) and granular chemical fertilizer (right). When placed on top of the soil, they dissolve gradually every time you water the plants.

Convenient Tools for Cultivation

Below are some useful tools for growing succulents

Shovels for soil
Used to fill the pot with soil. When you repot seedlings, you should use smaller pots, so it's recommended to have both a large and small shovel.

Gardening loves
Necessary when tending or replanting varieties with sharp spikes, such as agave. Gloves with a rubber palm are recommended.

Narrow-spout watering can
Necessary to avoid accidentally splashing water on leaves and stems.

Shower-type watering can
Used to water from above the leaves. Detachable shower mouths are convenient.

Scissors
Scissors are essential for taking appropriate care of succulents, for example when cutting off new bulbs, stems or old roots. It's recommended to have all three types of scissors shown above.

Label
Used to write the variety of your plant and keep track of the days when performed maintenance.

Blower
This tool was devised for blowing dust off camera lenses, but it can also be used for taking care of succulents, for example, to gently blow water from the leaves.

Cutter
Used to remove seedlings and roots. Any general cutter is more than sufficient; just have one that is convenient and easy to use.

Tweezers
These are useful for removing dead leaves or flowers, or filling gaps left in the soil when replanting.

Choosing a pot

Pots vary in ventilation and convenience of use depending on their composition. Unglazed pots have good ventilation and water evaporation, while plastic pots are lightweight, durable, and available in a wide range of sizes.

The size of the hole at the bottom of the pot also influences its drainage ability. Summer-type Caudices need warmth, so a darker pot that collects plenty of heat is ideal. Echeverias and other spring-fall varieties will do well in a wider range of pots, including white/light- colored ones. The timing of watering and amount of water required will slightly vary depending on the characteristics of each pot. So in general, always keep an eye on the condition of the soil and plants.

Plastic pots
They are lightweight and have good water retention and are available in various sizes.

Ceramic pots
They have good air permeability and get less steamy.

Tin pots
They are light, easy to handle and retain water. Choose ones with holes in the bottom, or drill your own holes.

Antique style pots
Popular because they look nice with succulents. Ceramic pots have good air permeability. Thicker ones retain water better.

Calendar for Cultivation

By growth type: Management Calendar

There are three main types of succulent plants: Summer type, Spring-Fall type and Winter type. Here are tips for keeping them strong and healthy!

Don't throw away the info label that was on the original pot.
When purchasing succulents, choose ones that have extensive information labels (including variety's name, genus, etc.) and keep the label for reference. If the plant doesn't have a label, it is a good idea to ask for this information when purchasing and take note of it.

Succulents have three growth-types (summer type, spring-fall type and winter type), each with a vigorous growth season, slow growth season and dormant season in different periods. Growth management is based on the growth type, but it is important to know the names and genus correctly, as different varieties may look similar but be in a completely different genus. The growth type is based on the temperatures of the succulent plant's native habitat during the growth season. It is important to remember that a summer type plant is not necessarily strong in hot weather, and a winter type plant is not necessarily strong in cold weather.

Spring-Fall type

Typical varieties:

| Adromischus (cooperi) | Echeveria (laui) | Crassula (capitella) | Haworthia (tsukikage) |

Growth Period

Spring and fall, the optimal temperature is 50-75°F/10-25°C

Watering

Water generously once the soil is dry. Growth is slow in summer and they go dormant during winter. Water sparingly in midsummer and once a month in winter.

Environment

Since they naturally grow on tropical/subtropical plateaus where summers are not very hot, they are susceptible to the high heat and humidity that are typical of summer in some regions. Special care is required in midsummer.

	Jan	Feb	Mar	Apr	May	Jun	Jul	Aug	Sep	Oct	Nov	Dec
Placement	In the sun, good ventilation (move indoors if under 34°F/1°C)			In the sun, good ventilation			Half-shade, good ventilation (make sure to avoid rain)			In the sun, good ventilation		
Watering	Water once or twice a month until the soil is half-moist		Gradually increase frequency	Water generously when the soil is dry		Gradually increase frequency	Once every 10 days, until the soil is half moist		Water generously when the soil is dry		Water once or twice a month until the soil is half-moist	
Fertilization			Fertilize once with slow-dissolving fertilizer		Fertilize once with slow-dissolving fertilizer				Fertilize once with slow-dissolving fertilizer (Don't do it if you want red foliage)			
Management			Period for repotting, dividing roots and other management						Period for replanting and dividing plants			

Summer type

Typical varieties:

Aloe (marlothii)

Agave (isthmensis)

Pachypodium (horombense)

Cactaceae (Mammillaria)

Growth Period

From Spring to fall, with a growth surge in summer, the optimal temperature is between 68–95°F/20 -35°C. It goes dormant in winter.

Watering

During the growth period, water generously when the soil is dry.

Environment

Many variants originally grew in arid tropical regions, so a fan or similar method is required to minimize high summer humidity. In winter, move the plants indoor in a bright setting before the temperatures go below 41°F/5°C.

	Jan	Feb	Mar	Apr	May	Jun	Jul	Aug	Sep	Oct	Nov	Dec
Placement	Indoors with good light and ventilation			Gradually move outdoors		In the sun, good ventilation				Move indoors before temperature drops below 41°F/5°C		
Watering	Do not water			Gradually start watering		Water generously when the soil is dry				Gradually reduce water amount	Do not water	
Fertilization						Slow-dissolving fertilizer once every two months						
Management						Optimal period for replanting and dividing.						

Winter type

Typical varieties:

Aeonium (Evening Glory)

Lithops (hallii)

Conophytum (uviforme)

Ihlenfeldtia (vanzylii)

Growth Period

Between fall and spring with a growth surge in colder months. It goes dormant during summer. They have a very different growth pattern from most plants and other succulent plants too.

Watering

From fall to spring, water generously once the soil is dry. Although they are winter type plants, reduce the frequency of watering during winter to avoid hindering their growth.

Environment

Move indoors when the minimum temperature drops below 34°F/1°C.

	Jan	Feb	Mar	Apr	May	Jun	Jul	Aug	Sep	Oct	Nov	Dec
Placement	Indoors with good light and ventilation		In the sun, good ventilation			In half-shade, good ventilation				In the sun, good ventilation	Move indoors when temperature drops below 34°F/1°C	
Watering	Water twice a month, until the soil is half-moist		Water generously when the soil is dry			Gradually reduce frequency of watering	Twice a month, just enough to moisten the surface of the soil		Gradually raise the frequency of watering	Water generously once the soil is dry	Twice a month, until the soil is half-moist	
Fertilization			Slow-dissolving Fertilizer once every two months							Slow-dissolving Fertilizer once every two months		
Management										Optimal period for replanting and dividing.		

How to Grow Succulents

Planting, Leafing, Repotting, Dividing

Succulents need to be managed in many ways as they grow, with roots outgrowing the pot and new sprouts growing often.

Let's manage our succulents!

Succulent plants have for long survived in harsh and arid environments; because of this, they grow differently from other plants; for example, they can produce offspring and smaller shoots from fallen leaves. As the plants grow, they change their appearance, with leaves growing longer and new sprouts emerging from the surface of the soil. Once the roots grow into the pot, repotting becomes necessary and, if you learn how to reuse sprouts and fallen leaves, you can easily increase the number of plants you have.

The best period of the year to plant or repot is in spring or fall. In summer, plants are more susceptible to bacteria and may grow weak, so avoid replanting during that period.

Tasks for various purposes

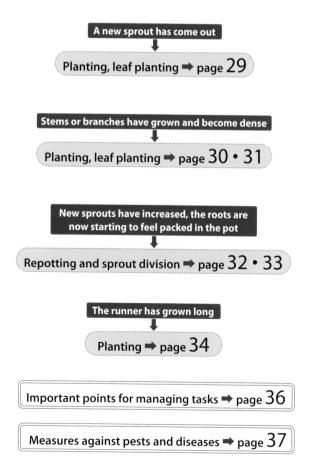

A new sprout has come out
↓
Planting, leaf planting ➡ page 29

Stems or branches have grown and become dense
↓
Planting, leaf planting ➡ page 30 • 31

New sprouts have increased, the roots are now starting to feel packed in the pot
↓
Repotting and sprout division ➡ page 32 • 33

The runner has grown long
↓
Planting ➡ page 34

Important points for managing tasks ➡ page 36

Measures against pests and diseases ➡ page 37

The leaves and stems are growing long and thin
↓
Planting ➡ page 35

How to clean up Conophytum & Lythops
↓
Removing the molten skin ➡ page 36

Flower buds are growing long
↓
Taking care of flower buds ➡ page 36

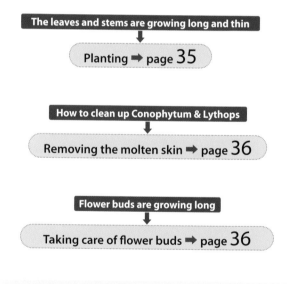

After repotting, wait a week before watering.

After repotting or tailoring a succulent plant, in general you want to wait 1 week before watering. Because these plants have evolved in a harsh natural environment, they will first try to get used to the new soil on their own. The plants may appear weak immediately after repotting, but they will gradually grow stronger and more resilient as they adjust to the new soil. This is why the first watering should be done about a week later.

CASE STUDY 1: A new sprout has come out!

There are many varieties of succulents that grow plenty of offspring, such as Echeveria, Sempervivum, Agave, Haworthia and many more. When you find new sprouts, you can cut them off and replant them to increase the number of plants you own.

Echeveria
(Echeveria
genus p.55)

Two sprouts have come out and the flower buds are growing longer.

Planting 1: Separating seedlings and planting

1 Cut the stems of the baby plants just below the soil surface

2 The stems should be at least ⅜"/1cm in length when placed in the soil.

3 Take time and consider how the leaves will appear when the sprout is replanted and the leaves spread out.

4 Cut the leaves a bit lower in relation to your mental image of the new plant and shape the plant up.

5 Shaped flower with the lower leaves removed.

6 Cut the flower buds, leaving an inch or so (2–3cm) in length.

7 Put the growths in a basket and let the cut ends dry out.

8 (1 month later) Once the dried-out cutting has sprouted, gently pull it out.

Graptoveria 'Margarete Reppin' (p. 72)

Depending on where and how many children (pups) are appearing, insert scissors carefully and avoid damaging the plant. After cutting the plant, you can proceed from step 4 above.
*See p. 72 for detailed instructions

When multiple sprouts appear at the same time

1 The stems are short and almost nonexistent.

2 If the stems are too short, you can cut a few leaves off.

3 You can also cut the young plants growing directly on the body of the parent plant.

9 Plant in dry soil. Wait one week before watering.

10 (2 months later) The new plant is now firmly rooted and growing well.

Leaf Insertion 1:

Place the leaves removed in steps 4 and 5 of the procedure above in a new pot, for leaf inserts. Place in a well-ventilated, semi-shaded location. Do not water until the roots start growing into the soil. Tip: Remove leaves by hand, not with scissors. Also, place them on top of the soil—don't bury them.

1 Separate the leaves of the cuttings.

2 Arrange the leaves on the soil. Note the date and plant type on your plant label.

CASE STUDY 2: Stems or branches have grown and become dense.

In varieties with branching and long stems, the overlapped foliage tends to lose light because of overgrown leaves. Thus, tailoring is required: while straightening and shaping up the plant, cut some parts of the leaves with consideration, so that the light can reach each branch.

Bronze Princess (Graptopetalum genus)

Branched stems grow in length and grow in a cluster.

Spring-Fall type

The bronze color gets darker during fall.

Planting 2: Cutting and tailoring longer leaf stalks

1 Cut stems so that a an inch or so (a few centimeters) is left.

2 Trim the stem.

3 Imagine the shape of the plant you want to grow and remove the unwanted leaves.

4 When removing leaves, make sure at least ⅜"/1cm of stem is left.

5 Put the cut ends in a basket to dry.

6 When the roots emerge, plant in dry soil.

7 (2 months later) The plant is firmly rooted and growing.

Leaf Insertion 2:

Some taller varieties can have their leaves taken and used for leaf insertion, while others may not be suitable. The Bronze Princess in the photo can be used, but there's only a 50% chance of the leaf growing into a full plant, so let's just hope for the best. Take the leaves removed in Step 4 above and place them on top of the soil. Place the leaves in half-shade with good ventilation and do not water them until they develop.

1 The leaves left from tailoring.

2 Arrange the leaves and insert a label with the type and name of the variety.

Varieties Ideal for Planting

The Aeonium genus (p. 40), Crassula genus (p.66), sedum genus (p. 78), Pachyphytum genus (p. 85) and various Stonecrop species work well with planting.

Teddy Bear (Kalanchoe p. 63)
You can remove the leaves easily by gently pulling and turning them.

Crassula 'Tom Thumb' (Crassula p. 70)
Position scissors below several branches clustered together and cut.

Cotyledon tomentosa (Cotyledon p. 77)
Cut the grown branches so that the light shines on all foliage.

Baby Finger (Pachyphytum p. 84)
Cut the tips, leaving few leaves on top.

Woolly Senecio
(Senecio p. 142)

It is a variety that takes a long time to grow, so let's be patient.

5 months later

The plant is firmly rooted and growing well.

Planting 3: Cutting leaves and stems to propagate

1 Cut the leaf stalks while considering their shape when inserted in soil.

2 Cut leaf stalks.

3 Remove leaves so that about ⅜"/1cm of the stem is left.

4 Leaf stalk with the leaves removed.

5 Dry the cut end in a basket.

6 Apply some rooting agent to the leaf stalk to encourage rooting.

7 2 months later; roots haven't appeared yet.

8 3 months later; roots have begun to appear on one of the tips.

9 4 months later: roots have finally emerged.

10 It's easier to plant it using a pair of tweezers. Don't water until a week has passed.

Planting and Cultivating the Leaf Inserts

Once sprouts start to emerge from the leaves, plant the sprouts in the soil. Insert them in the soil so that the roots are hidden in the soil and water them only after the parent leaves have started to wither. The most suitable varieties for leaf inserts are Echeveria (p. 44), Graptopetalum (p. 74), Sedum (p. 78), and Pachyphytum (p. 85) and more. The representative variety of the Pachypodium genus (p. 85), called caudex, doesn't allow leaf insert growth.

Golden Glow (Sedum)

Clavata (Crassula)

Chemicals to Promote Rooting

Commercial rooting hormones are available from companies like Garden Safe, Bonide, Miracle-Gro, Hormex and others. These help all manner of plants (not just succulents) to root faster and healthier. They can be purchased at gardening stores, home centers, and online.

When using any chemicals, carefully read all accompanying instructions for use. Do not them on food crops unless the packaging specifically states that it's safe to do so, and avoid contact with eyes.

Dissolve the chemical in a small amount of water and apply it to the roots.

These products come typically in the form of a powder that you mix with water as needed.

CASE STUDY 3: New sprouts have increased, the roots are now starting to feel packed in the pot.

If the parent plant is surrounded by a bunch of younger plants and the roots are sticking out from the bottom of the pot, let's repot the plant and divide the parent and child plants into new arrangements. In general, you want to repot before the pot becomes too filled with roots, about once a year.

Filifera x Isthmensis (Agave p.130)

The top of the pot is full of younger plants and the roots are stuck.

↓

1 month later

The parent plant and each child plant have been planted in different pots with dry soil.

Summer type

The sharp spikes are derived from isthmensis.

Repotting and dividing/separating plants 1 (for Agave)

1 Gently push the sides of the pot to loosen the soil a bit.

2 Slightly tilt the pot and remove the plant.

3 Break off the soil with your fingers.

4 Reddish or thin roots are old roots.

5 Hold the base of the roots and shake the plant little by little and remove/separate the child plants.

6 Remove each child plant, being careful not to break the tangled roots.

7 Remove older leaves from the parent plant, as they may cause rot later on. Keep the white and thick roots, remove thin and reddish roots.

8 Parent and child plants after the roots have been separated.

Replanting and dividing plants of other varieties.

In addition to the plants listed here (Agave), you can also replant and divide plants of many other varieties. Please refer to the specific pages for each variety for more detail about each variety.

Marin (Sempervivum p. 86)
As the roots are very thin, be careful when removing old roots.

Aloe rauhii (a.k.a. White Fox Aloe) (Aloe p. 92)
Use scissors to cut off old leaves.

Baylissiana (Gasteria p. 94)
The parent and child plants are easy to separate by holding both roots.

Picta
(Haworthia p. 103)

Child sprouts grow nicely if they have more than 7 leaves.

↓

After repotting

Repotting of the parent and child plants is complete.

In the case of Retusa (Haworthia)

This variety sprouts a huge amount of child sprouts and the roots are filling the pot. For repotting and dividing check p.104.

Repotting and dividing/separating plants 2 (for Haworthia)

1 Tap your wrist to shake and loosen the soil inside.

2 Gently squeeze the pot to loosen the soil a bit more.

3 Gently hold the plant and remove from the pot.

4 Tap your wrist to make the soil fall off the roots.

5 Remove old roots. Do not pull with too much force.

6 Old roots fall off easily, leave white roots as they are.

7 The roots after being cleaned.

8 Pull withered leaves with your fingers to remove them.

9 Remove old roots with tweezers.

10 Once old roots are cleaned out, the child plants and the parent plant will separate naturally.

11 Parent and child plants after being divided and cleaned up of old leaves and roots.

12 Soils to be used, left to right: pumice, Culture soil, decorative stones (small grain pumice).

13 Fill the pot with enough pumice stone to cover the bottom.

14 Next, add your culture soil. Place the plant in the right position and add soil.

15 Use tweezers or similar to fill the gaps in the soil.

16 The potted plant once the soil is properly placed.

17 The decorative stones prevent soil splatter and leaves from getting dirty and also prevent soil loss.

18 Potted plant complete with stones. In addition to keeping the soil in place and the leaves clean, stones can also prevent leaves from tearing.

CASE STUDY 4: The runners have grown long.

Some succulents have "runners," which are thin stems that grow into new shoots. In their native habitats, the shoots at the end of the runners reach the ground, take root, and multiply. In potted cultivation, the runners must be cut off and planted.

Orostachys
boehmeri
(Orostachys p.77)

Many runners are growing and the plant is getting weaker, with many withered leaves.

After repotting

The runners have just been planted. The first watering is in 1 week.

Planting 4: Cutting off runners and planting them

1 Cut the stem from about ⅜"/1cm below the leaves of the parent plant from which the runner has emerged.

2 Cut the runners to also give a neat and clean appearance to the parent plant.

3 Remove dead leaves from the cut runners and let them dry for about 3 days in half-shade.

4 Plant the runners in dry soil. Using tweezers makes this task easier.

How to plant Macdougallii (Graptopetalum p. 74)

1 Runners after being cut.

2 The thin stems from the runners should be planted facing the inside of the pot to grow in a nice shape.

Pinching off the growing point increases growth. (Aeonium p. 40)

1 Some Aeonium varieties produce new shoots when their growths are pinched off. In the photo, we show 'Emerald Ice' (p. 41)

3 Place in half-shade and care for the plant as usual.

2 The center part is the growing point. Remove the upper part along with leaves.

4 Three months later, several sprouts will grow from the parts you pinched off. You can increase the number of your plants by using this method.

CASE STUDY 5: The leaves and stems are growing long and thin.

Stems growing thin and wiry is also called "stretching." When stretching takes place, the plant is weakened and its resistance to pests, heat and cold is reduced. Since the plant can't return to its original state, it's best to trim it.

Sedum pachyphyllum (Sedum p. 81)

The stems are growing thin and long

Planting 5: Reviving and trimming stretched-out stems

1 Cut stems at a length that Is easy to reach. Cut above the parts that have hardened and become woody.

2 The stems have been cut. The parent plant will sprout again from the cut stems if it's placed in a sunny location.

3 Imagine the shape of the plants once replanted and lightly spread the leaves with your fingers.

4 Remove leaves by turning and pulling downward. Avoid peeling the stem's skin.

5 Stems with the leaves removed.

6 Dry the cut stems by placing them in a basket.

7 A month later, the roots have come out.

8 Plant in dry soil. Wait 1 week before watering.

Aeonium arboreum (Aeonium p. 40)

Even if the leaves and stems have gotten quite long, it's okay to trim and replant the plant.

Planting 6. Cutting off the stretched-out stems and trimming the plant

1 Cut off branches at a certain length. Young stems are more likely to start rooting. Leaving a branch on the original plant may encourage new growth as well.

2 After cutting. It is important that the cut end of the stock is green.

3 Dry the cut stems by placing them in a basket.

4 A month later, roots have come out.

5 Plant in a pot with dry soil.

6 Wait 1 week before watering.

How to cultivate while avoiding stretching.

In their native habitats, succulents have no blockage of sunlight whatsoever. They are exposed to plenty of sunlight and ventilation. When growing succulents, you have to keep in mind that your climate may differ in various ways and amounts, so it is important to create an environment as close as possible to your plant's natural one. As described earlier in "Basics of placement" (p.20), the key to a healthy succulent is placing the plant in a well-ventilated location outdoors, away from rain and in full sunlight to prevent stretching. Be careful to also follow seasonal watering and temperature control, and constantly check the condition of the leaves and stems while the plant is growing.

CASE STUDY 6: How to clean up Conophytum & Lythops.

Conophytum and Lithops grow in a molting cycle, with old leaves dying off as new leaves appear. When old leaves are left on the plant, they can cause damage to the plant, so be sure to remove them before they do.

Conophytum
tigozakura
(Conophytum p.120)

New shoots have sprouted and old leaves are withering.

Removing the molten residue

1 Being careful not to damage the leaves, remove withered parts with tweezers.

2 If there are any withering flower buds, remove those too.

3 You can remove withering flower buds by pulling them upward.

4 The plant after cleanup.

Winter-type They have a classic tabi (Japanese sock) shape and have bright pink flowers.

How to take care of flower buds.

Succulents have a variety of beautiful flowers, including red, pink, white, orange, yellow, and dotted flowers. The way they bloom is unique and varied, and some have long blooming periods. Once they wither, cut the flower stalks as soon as possible,

In the case of multifloral varieties that have many thick flower stalks, the parent plant itself may weaken if all the flowers bloom at once. If you want to encourage the growth of the parent plant, it is best to cut the flower stalks while they are still budding.

1 Haworthia cuspidate (Haworthia p. 99)

2 Cut a few centimeters from the stem of the flower.

3 After a while, the stem that was left will wither.

4 It can be removed easily with a gentle pull.

Tips for caring for your plants.

Time of the year

It is best to repot before the growth season. The ideal periods are spring and fall. When repotting, also clean the roots. It's not advisable to cut roots during the growth season however, and that is why it's best not to repot during that period. In case a repotting is unavoidable, be very careful when handling the roots.

Where to work on the plants

After trimming or cutting leaves, it is important that the cut ends dry out thoroughly. Place the plants in half-shade with good ventilation (as in the image at the lower right). This helps ensure that the cut end can dry out quickly.

The photo above shows an example of a cutting made with scissors that were not disinfected. The leaves are wrinkled and weak.

Disinfecting of equipment

Remember to clean all of your equipment before and after any work you do on your plants. It is especially important to disinfect scissors, both before and after using them and before changing from one plant variety to another, in order to prevent bacterial infections from cuts. Alcohol is an excellent disinfectant.

Watering

Do not water cuttings, young plants or leaves before they have rooted. Even after they've rooted and have been planted in the culture medium soil, wait a week before giving them their first watering.

Keep the cuttings dry.

Measures Against Pests and Disease

To protect succulents from pests and diseases, it is important to care for them accordingly to their growth type. When performing maintenance carefully observe your plants and make sure to act on any abnormalities.

Prevention and early detection
When it comes to pests, prevention and early detection are essential. As a basic rule, you should keep the plants in good sunlight and good ventilation, but be careful of overexposure and overwatering. Also, to avoid virus transmission from scissors and such, remember to sterilize tools with alcohol before and after each use.

Main pests

Worms
There are several types of worms and caterpillars that like succulent juices. If you find any, scrape them off with a soft brush and spray with a solution such as those pictured below (right). The plant pictured above is infected by bollworm.

Bollworm

Aphids
Pests that suck on plant juices. They reproduce quickly so get rid of them quickly before they multiply. Commercial insecticides work well, but diluted alcohol is a good alternative.

Slugs
Slugs like to hide under pots and eat plants during the night. Salt is damaging to plants, so don't use it. Stick to pesticides specifically targeting slugs and similar pests.

Red spider mites
Pests that suck on plant juices. They appear in spring once the weather gets warmer. They can be exterminated by spraying plenty of water, but it is more effective to use an anti-mite insecticide.

Injuries due to errors in care

Sunburn and leaf scorching
Leaving plants exposed to strong direct sunlight for a long period of time or suddenly moving greenhouse/indoor plants to an outdoor environment will cause leaf burn. If the burns are too severe, they will leave marks on the plant and eventually cause those parts to wither.

During periods of very strong sunlight, use shade nets and such to soften the light or move the plants to half-shade. When moving the plants from indoors to outdoors, it is important to get the plants gradually used to the new environment.

Root rot
When the pot starts getting full of roots and gets clogged, or when the pot is moist for a long period of time (due to excessive watering), the roots will start to rot and the rot may reach stems and leaves. If you notice rot, remove the rotten parts completely and completely dry out the cut ends and roots. Wait for new roots to emerge and then plant the sprouts in new, dry soil.

Pest control solutions

A mixture of neem oil and water or dish liquid and water are safe ways to remove pests. A light spraying of rubbing alcohol is also safe and effective. Neem oil is also a great fungicide. Avoid premixed neem oil, do a test application the first time you use any substance on your succulents, and avoid spraying your plants in full sunlight.

Insecticidal soaps are another safe option. Again, it's best to do a test application the first time you use it, and be sure to spay when plants are shaded (cooler times like early morning or evening are best).

There are many safe/organic treatments for pests and fungi. When choosing any product, bear in mind the presence of children and pets in your home. Check to ensure product safety, and always follow the instructions and cautions.

Main diseases

Soot (sooty mold)
Soot is a disease in which leaves and stems of plants are covered by black soot-like mold. Initially, the fungus grows in a black spot and it gradually spreads to cover the entire leaf or stem, inhibiting photosynthesis and suppressing growth.

This disease is caused by molds, which like to eat the excrements left by aphids and beetles. In fact, the mold itself does not grow on the plant, but instead grows on the pest excrements.

To prevent soot outbreaks, pests should be exterminated quickly when found. Also, to prevent diseases, keep the plant in a sunny and well-ventilated environment. And when the leaves and branches become overgrown, re-tailor or replant the succulents.

Bacterial soft rot
Soft rot is caused by bacteria that enters the stem, roots, or other parts of the plant. When a pest bites a leaf for example, bacteria are introduced inside the plant and start to multiply, causing the plant to rot and wither. Also, rotten plants emit a foul odor. If you use scissors on an infected plant, the infection will spread to other plants.

To prevent soft rot, follow these important steps: 1) cut off any diseased area immediately if found, 2) keep scissors, knives, tweezers, etc. clean and disinfected, 3) have an environment with good ventilation and sunlight to prevent the growth of bacteria, 4) manage and tend your plants (trimming and such) only on sunny days.

3

200 Popular Succulents

There are 60–70 different families of succulent plants growing over the world and it is said that there are more than 20 thousand varieties between gardening varieties and variants.

Varieties improve day by day, with new varieties being produced one after the other.

This section introduces 712 selected varieties of succulent plants. I have compiled detailed information for each species, including their growth types and tips for cultivation, from common species to popular and rare varieties.

(Note that some of the hybrids you will see in these pages were created in Japan or surrounding regions and therefore may be very uncommon outside of those areas.)

Aeonium
Crassulaceae genus

Place of Origin: Canary Islands, parts of North Africa
Growth Difficulty: 2/3
Type: Winter (some of them are Spring-Fall type)
Watering: In spring, fall and winter: water generously when the soil is dry. In mid-winter: reduce frequency. In summer: water a small amount few times a month.

Characteristics Aeonium evolved to tolerate drought in regions with very little rainfall. They are characterized by a flower-like rosette of leaves at the end of their long stems which grow upward like a tree trunk. The leaves vary in color from bright green, red, black-purple, and light yellow with thicker spots.

Tips for Cultivation Aeonium are sensitive to heat and sunlight: strong sunlight can easily cause leaf burn, so they should be placed in well-ventilated, half-shade environments during summer. In winter, when temperatures drop below 34°F/1°C, move them indoors.

Aeonium arboreum 'Luteovariegatum'

Aeonium arboreum 'Luteovariegatum' is one of the most popular arboreum varieties with beautiful pale, yellow-speckled pattern. It's medium in size and grows up to about 20"/50cm.

`Winter` `10 cm`

Aeonium arboreum 'Velour'

A cross between 'Zwartkop' and canariense (also called Canary Island Aeonium). The main difference from 'Zwartkop' is that the tips of the leaves are rounded. It's very cold-tolerant and can resist temperatures down to 28°F/-2°C.

`Winter` `13 cm`

Aeonium arboreum 'Zwartkop'

It has attractive, glossy, and dark, purple-colored leaves. It's weak to midwinter cold and should be moved indoors before temperatures drop below 34°F/1°C.

`Winter` `12 cm`

Aeonium 'Chocolate Tip'

It has lovely small rosette-shaped leaves. In winter, the dotted leaf pattern looks like chocolate chips.

`Winter` `12 cm`

Aeonium 'Copper Kettle'

Its name derives from its copper color. It is resistant to cold temperatures and can survive up to 27°F/ -3°C. Thus, it can be grown outdoors all year long in areas with light winds.

Winter **7 cm**

Aeonium decorum f. variegata

The beautiful foliage changes color each season. The new shoots are pale yellow, and the edges of the leaves turn red during the growth period. It is very sensitive to cold, so keep this variety indoors during winter.

Winter **11 cm**

Aeonium domesticum f. variegata

It is one of the most popular Aeoniums with many beautiful new sprouts. In summer it should be kept in half-shade to avoid leaf burn.

Winter **11 cm**

Aeonium 'Emerald Ice'

It has yellowish-green leaves with light colored edges and it grows into a beautiful rosette. The leaves don't turn red.

Winter **8 cm**

Aeonium sedifolium

The scientific name quite literally means "sedum-like leaves." It has plump looking leaves that grow in clusters. Water even during the dormant season, whenever the soil is dry.

Winter **8 cm**

Aeonium tabuliforme var. minima

This variety is weak to humidity, so it requires more ventilation than other succulents. Water once or twice a month, just enough to moisten the surface of the soil.

Winter **12 cm**

Adromischus
Crassulaceae genus

Place of Origin: North Africa, Namibia, etc.
Growth Difficulty: 1/3
Type: Spring-Fall
Watering: Water generously when the soil dries out. Do not water in summer, reduce frequency in winter.

Characteristics They have attractive plump and puffy leaves with very unique patterns. There are many small varieties that are about 4"/10cm tall and grow very slowly. The environment in which they grow influences leaf pattern and colors. The leaves are easily removed, but also root very easily when placed on soil.

Tips for Cultivation Since they naturally grow in desert areas, you want to keep them dry all year long. They need special care in summer during their dormant period. In winter, when temperatures drop below 41°F/5°C, move them indoors in front of a bright window.

Adromischus bolusii

The thick and fleshy speckled leaves grow red during fall. It grows very slowly.

Spring-Fall **8 cm**

Adromischus cooperi

Thick leaves with wavy leaf tips with a speckled pattern. Cooperi is a smaller species with round leaves.

Spring-Fall **8 cm**

Adromischus cristatus

Spring-Fall **8 cm**

It has wavy leaves and no speckled pattern. Thin sprouts develop on the stem as it grows.

Adromischus cristatus var. clavifolius

Spring-Fall **8 cm**

The tips of the leaves look like spatulas. The hairy part of the stem grows into a longer trunk.

Adromischus cristatus *Indian Clubs*

Spring-Fall **10 cm**

Its name comes from the juggling-pin-shaped club used for weight training. It's weak to high summer temperatures and humidity.

Adromischus filicaulis

It has pale green leaves with red and purple spots. Keep in half-shade during summer but in full sunlight in spring and fall.

Spring-Fall **8 cm**

Adromischus hemisphaericus

It has many oval leaves with tips pointing in various directions. The leaves fall off easily but also grow roots easily when placed on soil.

Spring-Fall **8 cm**

Adromischus marianiae *'Bryan Makin'*

It has green leaves with reddish spots, a typical pattern of Adromischus. The leaves are smallish and the stems grow in nice trunks.

Spring-Fall **8 cm**

Adromischus marianiae var. herrei *'Red Dorian'*

It has impressive reddish-brown rugged leaves. This plant is a slow grower. Do not water in midsummer and midwinter.

Spring-Fall **10 cm**

Adromischus marianiae var. antidorcatum

The plump leaves have a very unique reddish-brown dotted pattern that is typical of the Adromischus genus.

Spring-Fall **8 cm**

Adromischus trigynus

The brown spots on the flat, green leaves are unique to trigynus. The leaves detach easily, so be careful when repotting.

Spring-Fall **8 cm**

Echeveria
Crassulaceae genus

Place of Origin: Highlands in Mexico and Central America
Growth Difficulty: 3/3
Type: Spring-Fall
Watering: Leaving water in the central part of the plants causes leaf damage, so use a blower (p. 25). In winter, stop watering when the temperature drops below 32°F/0°C.

Characteristics The leaves form a rosette shape that looks a lot like a rose flower. It is a popular genus with a variety of leaves with beautiful colored and shaped leaves, also having varying leave borders. Many of the varieties turn red between fall and spring. There is a wide variety of species going from natural varieties to hybrid ones.

Tips for Cultivation In their native habitat, the average maximum temperature only goes as high as 77°F/25°C, so they are extremely weak to hot and humid summers. It is important to expose them to sunlight, but during summer it is best to keep them in half-shade or use shade nets and fans to create a very cool environment.

Echeveria affinis

It is popular for its chic, deep reddish-purple leaves. Keep in half-shade as it is sensitive to summer UV light. Beautiful deep red blooms.

Spring-Fall   **8 cm**

Echeveria agavoides x pulidonis

It has thick, spatula-like leaves with red edges around the tips. It's a hybrid between Echeveria agavoides and Echeveria pulidonis.

Spring-Fall   **12 cm**

Echeveria agavoides 'Ebony' x 'Mexican Giant'

A hybrid between Echeveria agavoides 'Ebony' and Mexican Giant'. The leaves have very sharp claw-like tips.

Spring-Fall   **10 cm**

Echeveria 'Alba Beauty'

It has rounded, elegant, pale leaves of a slight bluish green color. The leaf tips and edges may be pink.

Spring-Fall   **8 cm**

Echeveria 'Alfred'

Spring-Fall | **8 cm**

It has pink "nails" and transparent-looking skin. It is a hybrid of Echeveria pulidonis and albicans.

Echeveria 'Allegra'

Spring-Fall | **8 cm**

Its leaves are arranged in a rosette that points upward and faces inwards, making the plant look like it's standing. Be careful of high humidity.

Echeveria 'Apus'

Spring-Fall | **10 cm**

It's a hybrid between Echeveria pulidonis and Lindzeana, with red edges. It's also known as Aepus.

Echeveria 'Ariel'

Spring-Fall | **8 cm**

It has rounded and light green leaves with pink tints. When the leaves turn red in fall, the whole stem turns pink as well.

Echeveria 'Fall Flame'

Spring-Fall | **15 cm**

A unique and attractive plant with a gradation going from green at the base to deep crimson at the tips of its undulate leaves.

Echeveria 'Avocado Cream'

Spring-Fall | **8 cm**

The thick, plump, pink leaves have a somewhat hand-painted look. They are very pretty and popular.

Echeveria 'Bambino'

This a hybrid derived from laui (p.52) has beautiful white and powdery leave with orange flowers.

Spring-Fall | **15 cm**

Echeveria 'Baron Bold'

Spring-Fall | **11 cm**

This a variety has thick bumps on its leaves. The reddened leaves and the green center give it a mysterious charm.

Echeveria 'Ben Badis'

Spring-Fall | **8 cm**

The leaves are beautiful with a bright red color on the edges and tips of the leaves. It often produces clusters of young sprouts.

Echeveria *'Bini-ouhikou'*

Spring-Fall **8 cm**

The red tips and glossy leaves are the main feature of this variety. It has no stem, so only water the soil around it to avoid damage from moisture.

Echeveria *'Blue Cloud'*

Spring-Fall **10 cm**

It has elegant pale, white powdery leaves. Water the soil around the plant and avoid getting water on the leaves.

Echeveria *'Blue Orion'*

Spring-Fall **8 cm**

One of the most popular succulent varieties, with beautiful contrasts between the blue-tinged leaves and the red coloring on the tips and edges.

Echeveria *'Blue Sky'*

Spring-Fall **8 cm**

The rosette shape faces upward and gives a fresh impression as if it's looking right at the sky. It is one of the coolest-looking varieties with red edges.

Echeveria *'Blue Thunder'*

Spring-Fall **10 cm**

The white powder that covers the leaves gives a very powerful look that is unique to 'Mexican Giant' hybrids.

Echeveria *'Brown Rose'*

Spring-Fall **8 cm**

It has thick leaves protected by fine hairs. It has no stem, so only water the soil around it to avoid damage from moisture.

Echeveria *'Caribbean Cruise'*

Spring-Fall **8 cm**

Its leaves are reddish in color on the edges. If water droplets fall on the leaves, blow them away with a blower.

Echeveria *'Cherry Queen'*

Spring-Fall **10 cm**

Its leaves have a subtle light pink tint. Water the soil around the plant to avoid ruining its white powder.

Echeveria *'Crimson Tide'*

Spring-Fall **14 cm**

It has large wavy leaves that look like frills. This variety becomes red in fall so check p.53 for management tips.

Echeveria 'Christmas Eve'

Spring-Fall **8 cm**

The red edges on these leaves can take up a considerable amount of surface, making for a very colorful, eye-catching plant. It makes a great accent in a mixed arrangement.

Echeveria 'Chroma'

Spring-Fall **8 cm**

It's a standing-trunk type of succulent with small rosettes at the end. The leaves can be hard or bumpy depending on the season.

Echeveria 'Clara'

Spring-Fall **8 cm**

It has plump green leaves arranged in neat rows. In fall it changes to a pale reddish-purple color.

Echeveria 'Cloud'

Spring-Fall **8 cm**

This is one of the varieties that has opposite/inverted edges. The creamy green leaves are covered in gentle white powder.

Echeveria 'Cloud' f. monstrosa

Spring-Fall **8 cm**

The plant on the right side of the pot has petrified.

Echeveria 'Crystal Land'

Spring-Fall **10 cm**

It is unknown which gene gives it this film-like appearance. It is a hybrid of 'Crystal' and 'Mexican Giant'.

NOTE

Petrification (monstrosa) and Cresting (cristata)

Petrification
Echeveria 'Cloud'. You can see the heads splitting at the growth point.

Cresting
Euphorbia lactea 'Cristata'. The lactea usually has a white powdery look (p.111).

There is a phenomenon in plants called "fasciation," a deformity that causes tissues on the growing points to mutate and divide or multiply repeatedly in an unusual way. The final result is a mysterious shape that is very different from the original plant. It's seen most frequently in plants like foxgloves and strawberries. Succulents are very susceptible to fasciation. There are two types of fasciation that can occur: petrification and cresting.

Petrification happens when the plant repeatedly divides the growth point and forms new rosettes.

Cresting happens when the growth when damage causes the growing point to multiply, generally growing in cluster or band, creating a wavy shape. In scientific names, "monstrosa" refers to petrified and "cristata" refers to crested plants.

Echeveria *'Cubic Frost'*

Spring-Fall **10 cm**

A variety with thick, inverted leaves. The lower leaves tend to wither so remove them before they get moldy.

Echeveria *'Cubic Frost'* f. cristata

Spring-Fall **10 cm**

A uniquely deformed plant crested in a way that makes it hard to tell which parts of the plant have split and multiplied.

Echeveria cuspidata

Spring-Fall **8 cm**

It blooms multiple flowers at the same time. It weakens if all flowers are in bloom so cut some flower buds before they blossom.

Echeveria cuspidata var. *'Pink Zaragosa'*

Spring-Fall **10 cm**

It can have a very beautiful gradation going from creamy green to a bright pink on the leaf edges.

Echeveria cuspidata var. zaragozae hyb.

Spring-Fall **8 cm**

It grows reddish tips. The lovely orange flowers are typical of Echeveria.

Echeveria *'Debbi'*

Spring-Fall **8 cm**

This leaf color may attract beetles, so check for pests frequently. The leaf color changes to deep pink during winter.

Echeveria derenbergii

Spring-Fall **8 cm**

It has an elegant color and a well-defined shape to the rosette. It's one of the main representatives of smaller echeverias. It's also used for many hybrid variants.

Echeveria *'Derenceana'*

Spring-Fall **10 cm**

It gives off a very elegant look. It also looks very similar to its sister hybrid variety 'Lola'.

Echeveria *'Derosa'*

Spring-Fall **8 cm**

Its main feature is its glossy leaves. It has no stem, and grows in clusters, so be careful when watering to avoid damage from moisture.

Echeveria 'Dick's Pink'

`Spring-Fall` `11 cm`

It has large, rough leaves that are vertical but do not spread. Keep it in good sunlight for it to grow in a nice shape.

Echeveria 'Dondo'

`Spring-Fall` `10 cm`

The broad-tipped leaves have white powder on the underside. It grows very densely, so use a narrow-spout watering can.

Echeveria 'Dusty Rose'

`Spring-Fall` `8 cm`

As the name suggests, the leaves turn a dusty purplish-rose color in winter. In summer, it goes back to its usual green color.

Echeveria elegans

`Spring-Fall` `10 cm`

The edge of its leaves is slightly translucent and lets light through in a beautiful way. It is the parent variety of many hybrids.

Echeveria elegans potosina

`Spring-Fall` `8 cm`

It is technically the same species as elegans. (It is just one of many elegans's many variants.)

Echeveria 'Elegans Blue'

It grows upward in a trunk. It grows better and taller when it has good access to sunlight.

`Spring-Fall`

`11 cm`

Echeveria 'Exotic'

`Spring-Fall` `8 cm`

It has healthy, vigorous leaves and combines the characteristics of its two parents, Laui and runyonii 'Topsy Turvy'. It has inverted curved leaf edges.

Echeveria 'Fabiola'

`Spring-Fall` `10 cm`

It grows in a stiff rosette shape. It is tough and easy to grow. It's a cross between Echeveria purpusorum and Echeveria derenbergii (p. 48)

Echeveria fasciculata

`Spring-Fall` `10 cm`

The leaves turn to a beautiful crimson shade from winter to spring. This is a large variety that grows up to 20"/50cm in height.

Echeveria 'Fiona'

Spring-Fall **12 cm**

It has reddish brown leaves covered in white powder. Water the soil surrounding the plant.

Echeveria 'Fire Lips'

Spring-Fall **8 cm**

The tip of the leaves turn a bright red color from winter to spring. It works great in mixed arrangements. It's weak to summer heat.

Echeveria 'Fire Pillar'

Spring-Fall **8 cm**

Its rounded, curved leaves turn red between winter and spring. To grow nice red foliage it keep in good sunlight and fertilize in fall.

Echeveria 'Fleur Blanc'

Spring-Fall **8 cm**

It has translucent green leaves. In winter, the tips turn a pretty pink color.

Echeveria 'Giant Blue'

Spring-Fall **12 cm**

Its pink tips grow more colorful in colder months. It grows outward as well as upward.

Echeveria 'Giant Blue' f. cristata

Spring-Fall **12 cm**

A unique variety with a mixture of cresting and petrification. Its petrification gives it a stunning appearance.

Echeveria 'Gilva-no-bara'

Spring-Fall **8 cm**

This plant is characterized by its spiky crimson tips. It's a small variety, and works well as a colorful accent when planted in mixed arrangements.

Echeveria 'Gorgon's Grotto'

It has a long trunk and rough, red leaves with deep pink caruncles. The rosettes can reach 12"/30cm in diameter.

Spring-Fall **14 cm**

Echeveria 'Gusto'

Spring-Fall **8 cm**

It grows in a compact rosette shape. Its thick, densely packed leaves can have a blue or gray tint mixed with the green. Don't allow water to settle into the leaves.

Echeveria 'Hakuhou'

Spring-Fall **10 cm**

Its broad leaves can vary in color, from the pink-tipped green pictured here, to yellow, to orange, in accordance with the season. A cross between Pallida and Laui (p. 52)

Echeveria 'Hana-no-soufuren'

Spring-Fall **8 cm**

It grows red in color during colder months and grows yellow flowers in spring. It grows multiple flowers at once, so it's best to remove some of the buds before they blossom.

Echeveria elegans hyb.

Spring-Fall **10 cm**

It has a beautiful rosette shape that spreads similarly to chrysanthemum flowers. It works both alone and in mixed arrangements.

Echeveria 'Heracles'

Spring-Fall **10 cm**

This plant has densely packed leaves and produces lovely yellow flowers. Bright light gives the leaves their pink tips and edges, and the waxy surface protects it from burn.

Echeveria humilis

Spring-Fall **8 cm**

It's a beautiful variety with half-translucent leaf tips. It works great in mixed arrangements.

Echeveria hyalina

Spring-Fall **8 cm**

Once known as a variant of elegans, it was identified as a separate species in 2017. Color can vary to lighter green with more prominently pink tips.

Echeveria 'Irish Mint'

Spring-Fall **8 cm**

It's a hybrid of derenbergii and 'Topsy Turvy'. It keeps its minty-green color year round.

Echeveria 'Ivory'

Spring-Fall **7 cm**

Its color can range from a pale bluish-green to bright pastel green, and its leaves are charmingly plump. It grows many new sprouts in clusters.

Echeveria 'Joan Daniel'

Spring-Fall **8 cm**

Its leaves have a velvety covering of fine hairs on the surface. The leaves are easily damaged by water, so be carefully to water only the soil.

Echeveria 'Jupiter'

Spring-Fall | **8 cm**

This plant has exceptionally graceful leaves. They are coated in a white powder that is easily disrupted, so handle with care and keep water off the leaves.

Echeveria 'Kessel-no-bara'

Spring-Fall | **8 cm**

Its parentage is mysterious, and the plant itself gives off a mysterious look. The leaves turn orange rather than red during colder months.

Echeveria laui

Spring-Fall | **10 cm**

She's the queen of white Echeveria, covered in white powder all over her form. She's used in many hybrids.

Echeveria 'Laurinze'

Spring-Fall | **10 cm**

It grows up to 10"/25cm in size. It gets its white powder from its laui genes. The red color spreads and deepens in the colder months.

Echeveria 'Linda Jean'

Spring-Fall | **10 cm**

The leaves turn a unique purple in colder months, in contrast to their pale reddish color in summer. It's very sensitive to direct sunlight, so keep in half-shade during summer.

Echeveria lindsayana × 'Mexican Giant'

Spring-Fall | **8 cm**

This hybrid between lindsayana (which is a variety of colorata) and 'Mexican Giant' combines arching leaves with strong color.

Echeveria 'Lola'

Spring-Fall | **8 cm**

It has beautiful sherbet green leaves. It grows offspring in clusters. It's a sister hybrid to 'Derenceana' (p.48).

Echeveria 'Lupin'

Spring-Fall | **8 cm**

Elegant with pink edges and white powder, which it inherits from laui. When the leaves on the bottom start to wither, carefully remove them.

Echeveria macdougallii

Spring-Fall | **9 cm**

It has a 1.5"/4cm rosette at the tip of a long trunk. The tips of the leaves turn red in winter. Use this variety for accent in mixed arrangements.

Echeveria *'Minibelle'*

Spring-Fall **8 cm**

It grows up to 8–12"/20–30cm in height and the trunks woodify. The tips of the leaves turn red in winter. It also blossoms orange flowers.

Echeveria *'Momotarou'*

Spring-Fall **10 cm**

This plant can vary from the green you see here to a soft porcelain blue, and the berry-red color can dominate the tips and edges of the leaves.

Echeveria *'Moon Gadnis'*

Spring-Fall **8 cm**

The pink-tipped leaves form a lovely "cup" toward the top. Slow-growing, but can grow quite large. Also called 'Moon Goddess'.

Echeveria *'Mosan'*

Spring-Fall **8 cm**

It's a popular variety that has rounded leaves that turn pink in colder months and form a sturdy rosette. It produces yellow flowers.

Echeveria *'Murasakihigasa'*

Spring-Fall **8 cm**

It has many small rosettes that grow on the tips of stems and trunks. Its leaves turn orange in fall.

How to produce beautiful red fall foliage

NOTE

Color variation during colder months is common in Spring-Fall type succulents such as Echeverias and Crassulas. They are unique in that their leaves turn to their original color without falling. The keys to enjoying nice color changes are fertilization, sunlight and temperature.

▪ Do not fertilize in fall (check p. 26)

▪ Keep them outdoors from the beginning of fall until early spring and expose them to good sunlight.

▪ In order for the leaves to change color, cold temperatures are required, so in general, keep the succulents outside as much as possible but move them indoors when the minimum temperature drops below 32°F/0°C.

The color will return to normal as the temperatures rise again. Fertilize in March and May.

Echeveria *'Nagisa-no-yume'*

Spring-Fall **10 cm**

Its leaves are slightly hairy and are easily damaged by water. It's a hybrid of setosa var.minor.

Echeveria *'Nobara-no-sei'*

Spring-Fall **8 cm**

The leaf color remains the same all year round, but the tips turn red in winter. Its leaves have a high chance of rooting when detached.

Fall foliage in a Crassula (Fire Festival)

Echeveria *'Novahineriana'* × laui

Spring-Fall **8 cm**

It's a white echeveria with little red tips. It often grows new sprouts in clusters.

Echeveria *'Olivia'*

Spring-Fall **10 cm**

It has glossy leaves with spiky red tips. It could be also considered a member of the Graptobelia genus.

Echeveria *'Omoide-tsuyu'*

Spring-Fall **8 cm**

It is a hybrid of Echeveria prolifera and 'Derosa' (p.48). Its bright red foliage in winter makes it great as an accent for mixed arrangements.

Echeveria *'Onslow'*

Spring-Fall **8 cm**

It has muscat-colored leaves that turn pink in winter. It grows pink and orange flowers.

Echeveria *'Orion'*

Spring-Fall **10 cm**

It's one of the most common echeveria varieties, but its parentage is unknown. Its slightly pink leaves are its main characteristic.

Echeveria *'Ossein'*

Spring-Fall **8 cm**

Its green leaves have bright red edges. The leaves are very dense so be avoid high humidity and be careful when watering.

Echeveria *'Peach Pride'*

Spring-Fall **8 cm**

Its large and round leaves turn to a peach-like pink. Because of its soft appearance it's also referred to as princess of Echeverias.

Echeveria *'Peaches and Cream'*

Spring-Fall **10 cm**

It has flat and round leaves with pink edges. Also called 'Atlantis.'

Echeveria *'Peachmond'*

Spring-Fall **8 cm**

It has a small and thin shape and glossy muscat-colored leaves. Has a very elegant look.

Echeveria subsessilis

Spring-Fall | **10 cm**

Its bluish leaves don't change color, but the edges turn slightly pink. It's also called the Morning Beauty Plant

Echeveria *'Perle von Nürnberg'*

Spring-Fall | **10 cm**

Its leaves turn purple-pink in winter. It grows upward, so it is best to trim the trunk often.

Echeveria *'Piorisu'*

Spring-Fall | **10 cm**

It grows into a rosette of about 6"/15cm in length.

Echeveria *'Pixi'*

Spring-Fall | **10 cm**

It's a small echeveria with small blue-green leaves. It grows in clusters, so be careful of high humidity.

Echeveria *'Pretoria'*

Spring-Fall | **8 cm**

The tips of its leaves and the surrounding area turn pink during the colder months, giving it a lovely appearance.

Echeveria pringlei var. parva

Spring-Fall | **12 cm**

In early winter, the tips of the leaves turn a deep red. It has orange flowers and small rosettes.

Echeveria *'Prism'*

Spring-Fall | **8 cm**

The rosette has densely-packed overlapping leaves in the center, which gradually open up. The plant produces new sprouts at a very fast pace.

Echeveria pulidonis

Spring-Fall | **8 cm**

The color of its leaves, the red edges, and the well-shaped rosette form make it a perfect echeveria. It's the parent variant to many hybrids.

Echeveria pulidonis × *'Baby Finger'*

Spring-Fall | **8 cm**

The leaf shape of 'Baby Finger' and the basic rosette form of pulidonis give this plant the best of both worlds.

Echeveria pulvinata *'Frosty'*

Spring-Fall **10 cm**

It has beautiful velvety leaves covered in delicate hairs. It grows upward, so it should be trimmed often.

Echeveria pulvinata *'Ruby'*

Spring-Fall **12 cm**

It has beautiful velvety leaves that turn bright red in the colder months.

Echeveria *'Purple Princess'*

Spring-Fall **8 cm**

It has beautiful rosettes of spoon-like leaves. Water carefully to prevent water from collecting on the leaves.

Echeveria *'Ramillete'*

Spring-Fall **8 cm**

It has apple green leaves that turn orange in winter. Makes for a good accent color in mixed arrangements.

Echeveria *'Ramillete'* f. cristata

Spring-Fall **10 cm**

A crested variant of Echeveria 'Ramillete'.

Echeveria *'Rezry'*

Spring-Fall **8 cm**

It has a rosette shape with slender leaves lined up like petals. The leaves turn to a light purple in colder months and look a lot like real flowers.

Echeveria *'Riga'*

Spring-Fall **8 cm**

It has a beautiful edges that are ruby-pink in color. It has no stem, so water the soil around it to avoid damage from moisture.

Echeveria *'Riga'* var.

Spring-Fall **12 cm**

There are some variants of Echeveria 'Riga' that grow large stems similar to caudex (p.19).

Echeveria agavoides *'Romeo Rubin'*

Spring-Fall **6 cm**

The ruby red of this plant is exceptionally vibrant. The plant is sensitive to direct sunlight so keep in half-shade in midsummer.

Echeveria 'Rondorbin'

Spring-Fall | **9 cm**

Its slightly hairy leaves turn a light orange color in winter. Grows very much like a tree with branches.

Echeveria 'Rosularis'

Spring-Fall | **8 cm**

Its leaves uniquely curl inward like a spoon. It has orange flowers, typical of the Echeveria genus.

Echeveria 'Ruby Nova'

Spring-Fall | **10 cm**

Its leaves turn to a clear yellow color in winter, with the red edges maintaining their color. It also produces yellow flowers.

Echeveria 'San Luis'

Spring-Fall | **8 cm**

It has a beautiful rosette of spatula-like leaves with red tips and undersides. Its scientific name has not yet been settled upon.

Echeveria 'Sara Himebotan'

Spring-Fall | **8 cm**

As the temperature drops, the underside of its leaves gradually turns purple. The color can be intense and the gradation is graceful.

Echeveria 'Scarlet'

Spring-Fall | **8 cm**

It has a beautiful rosette shape with plump, densely overlapping leaves. It grows many new sprouts in clusters.

Echeveria 'Selena'

Spring-Fall | **8 cm**

It has long and narrow, sword-like leaves with reddish purple tips. Its yellow flowers are typical of Echeveria.

Echeveria 'Sensepurupu'

Spring-Fall | **8 cm**

It's a hybrid of purpusorum. It grows in a slightly larger rosette and has a strong presence.

Echeveria 'Shanson'

Spring-Fall | **7 cm**

It has muscat green leaves that turn orange in winter. The leaves have a lovely translucency.

Echeveria secunda 'Shichifuku-jin'

Spring-Fall **12 cm**

This plant is said to have been imported to Japan during the Meiji period and could be seen growing in clusters under the eaves of many houses.

Echeveria secunda f. cristata

Spring-Fall **8 cm**

It's a crested variant of Echeveria secunda, of which there are many varieties and sub-species. Its bluish leaves give an elegant impression.

Echeveria rundelli

Spring-Fall **8 cm**

A dense rosette with short hairs on its leaf tips. It's sensitive to heat, and will turn a rosy pink when exposed to intense sunlight and dryness.

Echeveria setosa var. minor

Spring-Fall **8 cm**

This is the closest variant to the original setosa in the setosa family. The underside of its leaves turn purple in colder months. It's sensitive to heat.

Echeveria 'Shimoyama Colorata'

Spring-Fall **10 cm**

Owing to similarity of characteristics, this is considered to be a variety of the colorata family, but it's not confirmed.

Echeveria 'Shirayukihime'

Spring-Fall **8 cm**

It has pinkish leaves covered in white powder. It is believed to be a hybrid between pulidonis (p.55) and elegans (p.49).

PETIT

Obtaining Succulents: Cutting the trunk (arrow), planting and tailoring

Echeveria 'Shichifuku-jin'

When you want to replant a succulent or cactus with a trunk, you can do it by cutting the trunk. The key is to keep the cut wound in the shade, let the cut end dry thoroughly, and wait patiently for new roots to develop.

1 Month later

1 The pot is full of new rosettes, with the offspring sprouting around the parent plant.

2 Cut off the parent plant with scissors, choose an adequate scissor size that can cut even the thickest trunks.

3 Leave ⅜ -⅕ "/ 1 - 1.5 cm of the stem for rooting and planting.

4 Place the cut parent plant in a glass jar or similar container and keep it in a shady, well-ventilated place to dry the cut end.

5 When the roots emerge, put the parent plant in a pot with dry culture medium soil.

Echeveria 'Silver Pop'

Spring-Fall | **8 cm**

It has chic claw-like leaf tips, giving it a classy look. Good for light-colored mixed arrangements.

Echeveria 'Snow Bunny'

Spring-Fall | **8 cm**

It has a beautiful rosette shape opening from the center. Only water the soil around the rosette to avoid white powder coming off the leaves.

Echeveria sp. Sauvcorimbosa

Spring-Fall | **8 cm**

Its leaves turn to a pale pink color in winter. The long leaves make for a good accent in mixed arrangements.

Echeveria 'Spectabilis'

Spring-Fall | **8 cm**

The leaves turn deep pink during the winter foliage season. The spreading rosettes make it a good main plant for mixed arrangements.

Echeveria subcorymbosa 'Lau 030'

Spring-Fall | **10 cm**

The short stems often spawn new sprouts and grow in dense clusters.

Echeveria 'Sumie'

Spring-Fall | **10 cm**

The elegant purple leaves turn pink in the colder seasons. The leaves have a pleasing lack of uniformity.

2 Months later

3 Months later

6 The roots are now firmly attached and the plant is growing.

7 The stem on the original plant the plant is covered by the child plants, now growing in place of the original parent plant.

8 The child plants have now grown large enough to be divided and replanted.

5 Months later

9 The replanted child plants are also growing. When new child sprouts appear, go back to the beginning of the first step. It is fun to give these as gifts to friends.

Echeveria 'Tippy'

Spring-Fall | **8 cm**

It has pale green leaves with pink tips. The underside of its leaves also turn pink during colder months. It works great in mixed arrangements of pinks and purples.

Echeveria turgida

It has thick leaves and spiky claw-like tips. Easily cultivated in warm, semi-shaded areas.

Spring-Fall

8 cm

Echeveria '*Victor*'

Spring-Fall **8 cm**

It grows into a trunk with extending branches. The rosettes at the end of its branches and the ruby-red edges resemble rose flowers.

Echeveria '*Water Lily*'

Spring-Fall **8 cm**

The pale bluish leaves fade closer to white during winter, giving it an elegant beauty.

Echeveria '*White Champagne*'

Spring-Fall **10 cm**

The Champagne variants have color variations such as pink and purple. The leaves turn red in colder months.

Echeveria '*White Ghost*'

Spring-Fall **8 cm**

The tips of its leaves are wavy and covered in white powder. It needs plenty of sunlight during its growth season to maintain health.

NOTE

Echeveria '*Yamatohime*'

Spring-Fall **8 cm**

It grows many small rosettes and spawns plenty of young sprouts. It is a multiflowered plant, so cut some away while they're still in bud.

Rules for naming new varieties

Succulent hybrid names

More and more hybrids are being created every day, at both the genus and species level.

A hybrid may simply be identified as "parent 1 x parent 2" or by its origin plant followed by the breeder's choice of a name, placed in single quotes, for example: Echeveria 'Morning Beauty'.

A few basic rules for hybrid nomenclature

1. Modifiers such as "pink" can't be used alone.
2. When two plants have been "mated" the mother's name appears first.
3. The origin plant name always precedes the breeder's "trademark."
4. When naming a hybrid, check to be sure the name hasn't been taken. Like all botanical names, each hybrid name is unique and universally recognized.

Echeveria 'Yamato-no-bara'

Spring-Fall | **8 cm**

The undersides of its leaves turn red when temperatures drop. The profusion of color makes a strong statement.

Echeveria 'Yukibina'

Spring-Fall | **10 cm**

Its leaves turn to a lighter color in winter. This coloring is not found in other varieties, which makes it unique. Keep in full sunlight during fall.

Echeveria 'Zaragozae Long Leaf'

Spring-Fall | **8 cm**

Displays the graceful, arching leaf form so often seen in long-leaf types. Keep in good sunlight to create a nice shape.

Echeveria hyb. 'Galacta'

Spring-Fall | **8 cm**

A hybrid derivate of 'Zaragozae'. The tips are highlighted by that hit of crimson.

Echeveria hyb. 'Sillans'

Spring-Fall | **8 cm**

It has cool muscat green leaves with pretty pink edges. It works well as an accent in mixed arrangements.

Echeveria hyb. 'Gilva'

Spring-Fall | **8 cm**

It has large leaves that beautifully overlap. Avoid letting water enter the crevices between leaves.

Echeveria hyb. 'Vashogozae'

Spring-Fall | **8 cm**

It has beautiful magenta pink flowers, but because it grows many flowers at once, cut a few to keep the plant from weakening.

Echeveria hyb. 'Halgen Billy'

Spring-Fall | **12 cm**

A smaller variant that produces many child sprouts in clusters. It has a characteristic spiky shape that can be easily recognized.

Echeveria hyb. 'Lila'

Spring-Fall | **8 cm**

A white to very pale green Echeveria. Its color stays about the same all year long.

Kalanchoe
Crassulaceae genus

Place of Origin: Madagascar, etc.
Growth Difficulty: 3/3
Type: Summer
Watering: During the growth season, water generously when the soil is dry. For varieties with fine hair, water the soil around the plant to avoid wetting the leaves. Be careful of long rainy periods.

Characteristics It's a genus that has unique foliage, with leaves and stems entirely covered in fine velvety hairs. Their leaves have many curves and form beautiful unique patterns. They also come in a variety of sizes, going from small plants to ones that are over 78"/2m in height.

Tips for Cultivation Being summer types, they should always be exposed to plenty of sunlight (avoid direct sunlight in mid-summer). Move indoors to a bright location when the minimum temperatures fall below 41°F/5°C and water very infrequently.

Kalanchoe beharensis

Summer | **11 cm**

Leaves with white fine hair. Grows similarly to a tree, but it can be re-tailored/trimmed so that it grows smaller.

Kalanchoe beharensis *'Fang'*

Summer | **11 cm**

The contrast between the fluffy hairs and the spikes on the underside of the leaves is attractive. It's susceptible to high humidity and should be kept in a dry place.

Kalanchoe beharensis *'Latiforia'*

Summer | **11 cm**

One of the many Kalanchoe beharensis variants. The leaves have large and wavy edges.

Kalanchoe longiflora var. coccinea

Summer | **8 cm**

The color contrast between the two sides of the leaves is beautiful. The difference in color especially stands out when exposed to full sun.

Kalanchoe nyikae

Summer | **8 cm**

The round, glossy, eaves gives this plant the nickname "Shovel Leaf" in the West and "Philosopher's Cup" in Japan. The leaves turn to a reddish-purple color in fall and winter.

Kalanchoe orgyalis

Summer | **8 cm**

The surface is covered with brown fine hairs, giving it a velvety texture. It is sensitive to cold temperatures.

Kalanchoe pumila

It has beautiful silver leaves covered with white powder. It grows upward similarly to a tree. It grows pink flowers in early spring.

Summer **11 cm**

Kalanchoe thyrsiflora

Green in summer, red in fall covered with white powder. The trunk grows upward. The plant grow small white flowers in late fall.

Summer **8 cm**

NOTE

Hybrid names and common names

You may have noticed from earlier pages that hybrids can be named for anything from the appearance of the plant to the name of someone significant in the creator's life. Some names are entirely mysterious. But choosing a name is a privilege that comes with creating a hybrid.

Many succulents, like other types of plants, have common names, some of which differ from one part of the world to the next. Because they can be so numerous, we have generally avoided using them in this guide, but it is worth acquainting yourself with their nicknames in your part of the world.

Kalanchoe orgyalis is called Copper Spoons in parts of the West. In Japan it is called Hermit's Dance.

PETIT

Obtaining Succulents: Cutting off growing stems or branches and re-tailoring

Kalanchoe 'Teddy Bear'

Summer   This is a slow-growing plant, so be patient.

1 Trim with the objective of improving exposure to sunlight and ventilation.

2 Remove leaves by gently pulling and turning.

3 After about 2 months, the roots have emerged.

4 The leaves have been planted and are now growing.

"Rabbit" Family

Fluffy and cute!

The Popular "Rabbit" family

Japan calls it the Rabbit Family, some western regions call it the Panda Plant—it's easy to see how both apply. The long, velvety, slender leaves of the tomentosa varieties of the Kalanchoe family do indeed look very much like rabbit ears, and the fuzzy surface and spotting are characteristic of the panda. Here are some of the members of the endearing "Rabbit family."

Summer   **10 cm**

The original species of the "Rabbit" family. It is essential to take measures against cold weather. Move them indoors to a bright spot before the minimum temperature falls below 41°F/5°C. The fine hairs covering the leaves protect the plant from strong sunlight. However, it is susceptible to high temperatures, high humidity, and direct sunlight in summer in Japan, so use shade nets or fans to control the heat.

Kalanchoe tomentosa *'Golden Girl'*

The hairs are a little more yellow colored compared to tomentosa.

Summer   **10 cm**

Kalanchoe tomentosa *'Nousagi'*

The leaves are shorter than those of Kalanchoe tomentosa, and both leaves and spots are generally darker in color.

Summer   **9 cm**

Kalanchoe tomentosa *'Dot Rabbit'*

The spots are darker and larger than those on tomentosa.

Summer **10 cm**

Kalanchoe tomentosa *'Panda Rabbit'*

It's very rare to find tomentosa species that grow flowers. It grows flowers that are also covered entirely in fine hairs.

Summer
10 cm

Kalanchoe tomentosa *'Giant'*

It's larger than other variants, with thicker leaves.

Summer **13 cm**

Kalanchoe tomentosa *'Chocolate Soldier'*

It turns to a beautiful chocolate color when exposed to full sun.

Summer **10 cm**

Kalanchoe tomentosa *'Cinnamon'*

A little more cinnamon-colored than tomentosa 'Chocolate Soldier'.

Summer
10 cm

Kalanchoe eriophylla

Grows in clusters rather than vertically (reaching about 4"/10cm in height). Covered whitish hairs. Produces lovely pink flowers.

Summer
11 cm

The "Rabbit" Family   65

Crassula
Crassulaceae genus

Place of Origin: Mainly Southern Africa
Growth Difficulty: 2/3
Type: There are three different growth patterns. Summer type, Spring-Fall type, Winter type
Watering: Depends on the growth type so make sure to check this when purchasing your plant.

Characteristics The popular small varieties are from habitats that have occasional rainfall in winter, other varieties are from habitats where rainfall is common year-round. A small subset of varieties are from habitats in which there is no rain all year long.

As the different varieties have grown in a large variety of habitats, their characteristics also vary.

Tips for Cultivation In general, place in sunny and well-ventilated places. Winter and Spring-Fall types go dormant in summer and are susceptible to high temperatures and humidity in mid-summer, so keep them in half-shade, away from direct sunlight. The Summer type Crassula varieties can be grown outdoors even when under rain.

Crassula capitella

It grows with overlapping small leaves and produces fragrant white flowers in spring.

Spring-Fall **8 cm**

Crassula capitella f. variegata

It has a beautiful salmon-pink color on new leaves near the growth points, acting as an antioxidant to protect the new shoots.

Spring-Fall **9 cm**

Crassula capitella *'Campfire'*

Spring-Fall **9 cm**

The red color gets brighter as the weather gets colder. It's cold and heat resistant and generally very hardy. It's a good accent for mixed arrangements.

Crassula capitella *'Campfire'* f. variegata

Spring-Fall **8 cm**

A spotted variety of 'Campfire'. It has yellow-green foliage with cream-colored spots and pink foliage in winter.

Crassula *'Blue Waves'*

Spring-Fall **8 cm**

The waxy, undulating leaves turn fuchsia in winter. As the plant grows (it can reach a height of about 12"/30cm) it becomes bonsai-like in appearance.

Crassula 'Celia'

Spring-Fall | **8 cm**

A rare species with unique overlapping leaves and plants that grow in clusters. New sprouts also grow in clusters.

Crassula clavata

Spring-Fall | **8 cm**

It turns beautiful colors when kept under good sunlight. It reproduces very easily, so it requires tailoring before the growing season.

Crassula cordata

Spring-Fall | **8 cm**

The curvy, elegant leaves give a very classy look. The flower stalks form bulbs that eventually fall off and start rooting.

Crassula 'David'

Spring-Fall | **8 cm**

It has small, plump leaves with fine needle-like hairs on the edges and underside. The leaves turn a deep red color in winter.

Crassula exilis ssp. cooperi

Spring-Fall | **11 cm**

The leaves have beautiful red dots and fine hairs, and the underside of the leaves is also deep red. It is susceptible to high temperatures, high humidity, and direct sunlight.

Crassula expansa ssp. fragilis

Spring-Fall | **10 cm**

Delicate-looking but actually very hardy, it makes a accent plant in mixed arrangements. It is susceptible to high temperatures and humidity.

Crassula 'Garnet Lotus'

Spring-Fall | **10 cm**

The white powdery leaves have a pale red color. It needs plenty of sunlight to bring out its full color potential.

Crassula hirsuta

Spring-Fall | **11 cm**

It grows in clusters with fine long, slender leaves. In spring, it produces small white flowers that grow on the tips of long flower stalks.

Crassula 'Red Pagoda'

Spring-Fall | **10 cm**

Its deep red leaves are beautiful, and it has a very exotic look to it, despite being a very common variety. The color contrast of the red leaves against the green base of the plant is striking.

Crassula *'Ivory Pagoda'*

Spring-Fall **10 cm**

Its leaves, which are covered with white hairs, grow in layers. It is susceptible to high temperatures and humidity, so keep it in a well-ventilated place.

Crassula lactea

Spring-Fall **8 cm**

Grows with a trunk and branches. It's sturdy and easy to grow. It grows fragrant white flowers in winter.

Crassula lycopodioides var. pseudoly-copodioides

Spring-Fall **8 cm**

It has small and scaly leaves. When the lower leaves fall off and the stems start to stand out, they can be replanted.

Crassula mesembrianthoides

Spring-Fall **11 cm**

The leaves look like small animal tails. The tips of the leaves turn red during fall. It can be used as an accent in a mixed arrangements.

Crassula *'Momiji Matsuri'*

Spring-Fall **8 cm**

Smaller than Crassula 'Campfire' (p. 66). The red leaves look magnificent in winter. For a more beautiful red color, use less fertilizer in fall.

Crassula muscosa

Spring-Fall **8 cm**

The black marks seen between the leaves are the traces left by flowers. In spring, star-shaped yellow flowers grow between the stems.

Crassula orbicularis

Spring-Fall **8 cm**

Crassula orbicularis produces runners and is a fun plant to propagate. In summer, it should be placed in a well-ventilated semi-shady area.

Crassula ovata sp. *'Hime Ougon Kagetsu'*

Spring-Fall **14 cm**

It's a variety of Crassula ovata, The red leaves on the edges are lovely.

Crassula pellucida ssp. marginalis *'Little Missy'*

Spring-Fall **8 cm**

The pink edges on the small leaves give this plant a dainty appearance. It is also perfect for a mixed arrangement.

Crassula perfoliata var. falcata

Spring-Fall | **8 cm**

A very attractive plant with sword-shaped leaves that are almost perpendicular to the stem. It's a hybrid variety with many different parents. It's susceptible to cold weather.

Crassula perfoliata var. falcata f. minor

Spring-Fall | **7 cm**

A variant with shorter leaves and rounded tips which give it a soft, gentle appearance.

Crassula perforata f. variegata

Spring-Fall | **8 cm**

The triangular leaves overlap each other alternately and grow upward. You can grow them in clusters by planting their shoots in soil.

Crassula portulacea f. variegata

Spring-Fall | **13 cm**

The leaves are beautifully colored, with deep red edges and varied patches that alter the edges' color. It is susceptible to leaf burn.

Crassula pruinosa

Spring-Fall | **12 cm**

The leaves are thin and silvery with a thin coating of white powder. It branches and grows in clusters, so it's susceptible to moisture. Be careful when watering.

Crassula pubescens

Spring-Fall | **10 cm**

It has small leaves covered in fine hairs. Avoid exposing it to direct sunlight in summer and be careful of high temperatures and humidity. Plenty of sunlight in spring and fall will give more vibrancy to its leaves.

Crassula pubescens ssp. radicans

Spring-Fall | **8 cm**

It grows multiple white flowers in early spring. Its leaves turn red in winter.

Crassula subaphylla (syn. Crassula remota)

Spring-Fall | **11 cm**

Also called Crassula remota. It has small almond-shaped leaves with fine hairs. A good choice for hanging-type arrangements.

Crassula rupestris ssp. marnieriana

Spring-Fall | **8 cm**

It has small, fleshy leaves that alternate from side to side. The red tinge can be confined to the edges or infuse the entire plant. The flowers tend to reach straight upward.

Crassula *'Pastel'*

Spring-Fall **8 cm**

A variant of Crassula 'Tom Thumb'. The small, light-colored leaves are lightly dotted. In spring, tiny white flowers top the leaf clusters.

Crassula rupestris sp. (Large form)

Spring-Fall **8 cm**

It's a large variant of rupestris with thick, triangular leaves that alternate from side to side. Its leaf edges turn red in fall and winter.

Crassula salmentosa f. variegata

Spring-Fall **10 cm**

This plant may not look like a succulent, but it is a member of the Crassula family. It grows rapidly and should be pruned between spring and early summer.

Crassula socialis sp. transvaal

Spring-Fall **8 cm**

The small leaves are full of fine hairs. In fall and winter, the color contrast between the reddish leaves and the white flowers is particularly intense.

Crassula susannae

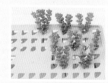

Spring-Fall **7 cm**

Its crunched leaves are unique. It produces new sprouts in clusters but grows very slowly. Requires patience.

Crassula *'Tom Thumb'*

Spring-Fall **10 cm**

It grows in clusters of small thick leaves. Its foliage in fall and winter looks like a pattern drawn by an artist.

Obtaining Succulents: Cutting off growing stems or branches and re-tailoring

PETIT

Crassula *'Tom Thumb'*

This plant can provide plenty of filler in arrangements. The long stems add movement, and they look great in wreathes as well.

1 Most branches split into two or three new, cut just below the split.

2 Looks nice and tidy after cutting

3 Remove the lower leaves and leave part of the stem "naked"

4 The leaves have been removed

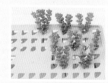

5 Put the cut ends in a basket to dry.

6 When the roots emerge, plant them in dry culture medium soil.

7 Two months later, the plant is growing well.

Graptoveria
Crassulaceae genus

Place of Origin: none (only hybrids)
Growth Difficulty: 3/3
Type: Spring-Fall
Watering: If water gathered in the plants center will damage it, so use a blower (p.25) to blow away any water droplets. In winter, stop watering when the temperatures drop below 32°F/0°C.

Characteristics It's a hybrid genus of Echeveria and Graptopetalum. It's stronger and easier to grow than pure Graptopetalum. The thick, rosette-shaped leaves are beautifully colored .

Tips for Cultivation In general, keep them exposed to good sunlight in a well-ventilated spot. Make sure they receive enough ventilation during rainy seasons and during summer, as they are very susceptible to humidity. Water generously when the soil's surface dries out.

Graptoveria 'A Grim One'

Spring-Fall | **8 cm**

There's nothing grim-looking about this plant, with its pastel-to-silvery green leaves and tight rosette formation. It produces orange-dotted yellow flowers.

Graptoveria 'Bashful'

Spring-Fall | **11 cm**

The "Bashful" in its scientific name implies that it's shy, but don't be fooled. The leaves turn bright red during fall and winter.

Graptoveria 'Bella'

Spring-Fall | **12 cm**

It has plump leaves growing in small rosettes. It grows beautiful flowers with a gradation going from yellow to red.

Graptoveria 'Decain'

Spring-Fall | **10 cm**

It has an unusual grayish-green leaf color that changes to an austere pink during fall and winter.

Graptoveria 'Huthspinke'

Spring-Fall | **11 cm**

The purplish leaves turn completely purple when it gets colder. It has a strong presence, so it can play a main role in a mixed arrangements.

Graptoveria 'Huthspinke' f. cristata

Spring-Fall | **12 cm**

A crested 'Huthspinke'. Instead of having a single growth point, it grows in an odd band-like shape.

Graptoveria *'Opalina'*

Spring-Fall **8 cm**

The leaves are large and plump. It is very strong and tolerates heat and cold well. Be careful not to overwater.

Graptoveria *'Pretty in Pink'*

Spring-Fall **8 cm**

Individual plants can range in the amount of pink they contain. Grows yellow flowers in early spring.

Graptoveria *'Purple Dream'*

Spring-Fall **8 cm**

The leaves turn to a vivid reddish-purple color when the weather gets colder. The small leaves and rounded shape of the plant make it convenient for mixed arrangements.

Graptoveria *'Rose Queen'*

Spring-Fall **11 cm**

After a few years of growth, red dots start appearing on the underside of the faintly peach-colored leaves.

Graptoveria *'Silver Star'*

Spring-Fall **8 cm**

The slender, pointed tips give it a unique appearance. The edges turn red in fall. It works well as an accent in mixed arrangements.

Graptoveria *'Titubans'* f. variegata

Spring-Fall **8 cm**

In winter, the leaves turn milky pink in the speckled parts. Creates a nice option for mixed arrangements.

Obtaining Succulents: Cutting off offspring sprouts and re-tailoring

PETIT

Graptoveria *'Margarete Reppin'*

Spring-Fall

Grows in clusters around a trunk. It's susceptible to humidity.

1 Cut off the abundant offspring and trim the plant.

2 Cutting off the offspring sprouts.

3 For shorter stems, cut so that a few leaves are left.

4 Remove the lower leaves so that the stem is about ⅜"/1 cm long.

5 Leave in a basket to dry.

6 When roots emerge, plant in dry culture medium soil.

Graptosedum

Crassulaceae genus

Place of Origin: None (hybrid)
Growth Difficulty: 3/3
Type: Spring-Fall **Watering:** When the soil dries out, water generously. Reduce watering during summer and winter.

Characteristics

It's a hybrid between Graptopetalum and Sedum. Many species are resistant to both hot and cold temperatures and can be grown outdoors year round in many regions. They are strong and easy to grow. The thick, rosette-shaped leaves also have a beautiful nuanced coloring, turning beautiful shades in fall.

Tips for Cultivation

In general, keep in a bright and well-ventilated place. Water generously when the soil dries out. While they are very strong varieties, they are susceptible to high humidity during the rainy season and summer, so reduce the watering frequency and keep them dry.

Graptosedum *'Little Beauty'*

Spring-Fall **8 cm**

In winter the tips of the leaves turn red, orange, and green. This tri- color gradation lends this plant's appearance a complete transformation.

Cremnosedum

Crassulaceae genus

Place of Origin: None (hybrid)
Growth Difficulty: 3/3
Type: Spring-Fall **Watering:** Water generously 2–3 days after the soil's surface dries out. Reduce watering during summer.

Characteristics

It is believed to be a hybrid between Clemnophila and Sedum (opinions on the parent genus are varied). In general it has the same characteristics as Sedum.

Tips for Cultivation

Basically the same as for Sedum. Grow in sunny and well-ventilated spots, avoid direct sunlight in summer by placing in half-shade. When they start growing offspring sprouts in clusters, replant them before the rainy season.

Cremnosedum *'Crocodile'*

The leaves are spiral-shaped, and the stem grows upward like a trunk. The stems can become very long, so it is best to trim them to maintain the shape of the tree.

Spring-Fall
8 cm

Cremnosedum *'Little Gem'*

It has glossy, triangular leaves that develop in a rosette shape. It produces yellow flowers in spring. It's susceptible to high summer temperatures and humidity.

Spring-Fall
10 cm

Graptopetalum
Crassulaceae genus

Place of Origin: Mexico, Central America.
Growth Difficulty: 3/3
Type: Spring-Fall but similar to Summer types
Watering: When the soil dries out, water generously. Reduce watering during summer and stop completely watering in winter.

Characteristics Most of the varieties are small with thick, small leaves in rosette shapes. The leaves of some varieties are covered in white powder, while others turn red in spring and fall. In general they are strong and easy to grow.

Tips for Cultivation They like direct sunlight and are relatively strong against heat and cold. They can be grown outside even during winter as long as care is taken to protect the leaves from freezing. If left growing in large clusters, they can accumulate moisture during the summer, causing rot, so be careful when watering, and make sure to separate parent plants from offspring.

Graptopetalum bellum

In contrast to the upward-reaching pink flowers, the bronze-green rosettes lie somewhat flat. Formerly known as Tacitus bellus.

Spring-Fall **10 cm**

Graptopetalum 'Daruma Shuurei'

It's elegant with light colors and plump leaves. It tends to grow in clumps, so it needs frequent care.

Spring-Fall **8 cm**

Graptopetalum pachyphyllum 'Blue Bean'

Spring-Fall **8 cm**

It has blue-gray leaves with dark purple spots at the tips. Water the soil around the plant to prevent the base from accumulating moisture.

Graptopetalum paraguayense

Spring-Fall **8 cm**

This vigorous plant produces offspring, sprouts from fallen leaves, creeps, and stands on its own trunk too. It is evergreen and is great for everything from hanging plants to groundcover.

Graptopetalum mendozae

Spring-Fall **8 cm**

The leaves turn pale pink when it gets cold and tend to fall off if the plant is subjected to high humidity for an extended period, so keep it dry.

Graptopetalum mendozae f. variegata

`Spring-Fall` `8 cm`

The leaves lose color around the edges, giving a pastel color to the entire plant. Works well as an accent in mixed arrangements.

Graptopetalum 'Pebbles'

`Spring-Fall` `10 cm`

The leaves turn a vivid purple color when the weather gets cold. It produces plenty of offspring. It's susceptible to high humidity.

Graptopetalum rusbyi

`Spring-Fall` `10 cm`

The austere color of this plant is an attractive, smoldering silver-purple. It grows in clusters of small rosettes.

Pachyveria
Crassulaceae genus

Place of Origin: None **Growth Difficulty:** 2/3
Type: Spring-Fall **Watering:** When the soil dries out, water generously. Reduce watering during summer and winter.

Characteristics It's a hybrid genus of pachyphytum and Echeveria. They have characteristic plump and round leaves covered with a faint white powder and beautiful colors underneath. They are resilient to cold weather and can be grown outside all year round in some areas.

Tips for Cultivation When it lacks sunlight, the leaves lose their characteristic color and grow unusually long. It's also susceptible to high humidity, so water sparingly during the rainy season or humid summers.

NOTE
/

What are hybrid genera? (intergeneric hybrids)

Hybrids are commonly made within parents of the same genus, but when plants from different genus/families are crossed, they inherit very different characteristics compared to their parent genera, forming "intergeneric hybrids."

As an example, Graptopetalum x Echeveria intergenetic hybrids are considered to be in the "Graptoveria family," which inherits various qualities from both of their parent genera.

Pachyveria 'Peach Girl'

`Spring-Fall` `8 cm`

From fall to spring, the leaves in the center of the plant turn to a peachy color, giving it a pretty appearance.

Cotyledon

Crassulaceae genus

Place of Origin: Southern Africa
Growth Difficulty: 3/3
Type: Spring-Fall
Watering: When the soil dries out, water generously. Reduce watering during summer and winter. For varieties with fine hairs, water the soil around the plant to avoid damaging the leaves. Be careful of rain drops in the rainy season.

Characteristics Many of them have charming shapes, like a bear's paw or a kitten's claw for example, with red edges on the leaves. The lower part of the stem turns brown and becomes woody.

Tips for Cultivation Most of them are resistant to both hot and cold weather (the speckled varieties are less resistant than regular ones), but it's good to avoid exposing them to direct sunlight in midsummer, moving them to half-shade instead. In winter, they go into dormancy so water them less frequently than in other season. In winter, you want to water when the leaves start losing their firmness.

Cotyledon campanulata

It has long and slender club-shaped leaves with fine hairs. The trunk grows quickly and it should be trimmed regularly by pruning or dividing the plant.

Summer **10 cm**

Cotyledon 'Hakubijin'

"White Beauty" is the Japanese name for this plant, and the slender white leaves truly are "white beauties." The tips of the leaves turn red during winter. It grows slowly and upward along its trunk.

Spring-Fall **13 cm**

Cotyledon orbiculata var. oophylla

The leaves have a brilliant look with pale white powder coating them and deep red edges. It grows orange bell-like flowers.

Spring-Fall **15 cm**

Cotyledon orbiculata 'Fukkura'

The plump, white-skinned foliage makes this plant calming to look at. It is prone to stretching, so be sure it's exposed to good sunlight.

Spring-Fall **9 cm**

Cotyledon orbiculata *'Peppermint'*

Spring-Fall | **8 cm**

One of the most powerful-looking Cotyledon orbiculata variants. The leaves become whiter as it grows.

Cotyledon *'Tinkerbell'*

Spring-Fall | **13 cm**

A bonsai-looking variety with small leaves and pretty orange flowers. It grows up to a height of about 12"/30 cm with a tree-like trunk.

Cotyledon tomentosa ssp. Ladismithensis *'Konekonotsume'*

Spring-Fall | **7 cm**

Has hairy, paw/claw-shaped leaves. The tiny flowers create quite a contrast. Water the soil around it, avoiding the leaves.

Orostachys
Crassulaceae genus

Place of Origin: Russia, China, Japan, etc. **Growth Difficulty:** 2/3
Type: Spring-Fall **Watering:** When the soil dries out, water generously. During its dormancy in winter, water only once a month.

Characteristics

A genus with as few as around ten varieties, it grows in Russia, China, Japan, Korea, and their immediate environs. The Iwarenge and Tsumerenge varieties are native to Japan. Orostachys are dense growers, but are not commonly found outside of their native environment. Their rosette forms are generally rounded, and quite graceful. After blossoming, the parent plant withers and produces offspring plants that are connected by stems under the surface of the soil.

Tips for Cultivation

They are strong to cold weather but they are weak against hot and humid summers so keep them in half-shade with good ventilation during summer.

Orostachys iwarenge var. boehmeri

The spoon-shaped leaves grow in a pretty rosette shape. It grows using runners and produces plenty of seedlings which makes it easy to increase in number.

Spring-Fall

8 cm

PETIT

Obtaining Succulents: Cutting off growing stems or branches and re-tailoring

Cotyledon tomentosa ssp. Ladismithensis

Cotyledons have a very low chance of rooting from their leaves, so let's trim and replant instead.

Spring-Fall

It's very susceptible to high temperatures and high humidity. Keep in half-shade during summer

1 Trim/prune once there are too many branches.

2 The ventilation has improved and sunlight can reach deeper into the plant.

3 Remove leaves so that ⅜–½"/1–1.5cm of stem is left.

4 Place the cutting in a basket or other container and allow the cut ends to dry.

5 It takes about 3 months for all the shoots to root. Cotyledons take a long time to root.

6 Plant in dry culture medium soil.

7 The plants are now growing well.

Sedum
Crassulaceae genus

Place of Origin: Various areas all over the world
Growth Difficulty: 3/3 (a small section is more difficult)
Type: Spring-Fall, Summer
Watering: When the soil dries out, water generously. During winter, reduce watering to only once a month and giving a more moderate amount of water than usual.

Characteristics There are plenty of Sedum varieties, including those with small puffy leaves, those that grow in rosettes, and others that grow in a necklace shape. Many of them have beautiful red leaves as their main characteristic.

Tips for Cultivation Keep them outdoors somewhere with plenty of sunlight and good ventilation. They are weak to direct sunlight in midsummer, so keep them in half-shade or cover them with shade nets. Be careful as they also grow in clusters which makes them susceptible to humidity. In winter, keep them dry to prevent the leaves from freezing.

Sedum acre *'Elegans'*

The tips of the leaves turn a bright creamy yellow during the growth period in spring and return to green as they grow more. It works well in groundcover arrangements and as accents in mixed arrangements.

Spring-Fall   **8 cm**

Sedum adolphi

Glossy yellow-green foliage with a trunk that grows tree-like branches. Its leaves turn slightly orange in fall and winter. Very hardy and easy to grow.

Spring-Fall   **8 cm**

Sedum adolphi *'Golden Glow'*

The leaves turn yellow to bright orange in midwinter. It works well in the back rows of mixed arrangements as the trunk will grow and stand out.

Spring-Fall   **8 cm**

Sedum album *'Blackberry'*

It's the album variant with the darkest color during midwinter. It has with small, narrow, rounded leaves. A chic touch in sophisticated mixed arrangements.

Spring-Fall   **8 cm**

Sedum album *'Coral Carpet'*

Spring-Fall | **10 cm**

It's green from spring to fall but turns coral-red when temperatures drop. It grows white flowers in early summer.

Sedum album *'Hillebrandtii'*

Spring-Fall | **8 cm**

Its leaves are slightly larger than other album variants and turn brown in winter.

Sedum corynephyllum

Spring-Fall | **13 cm**

The lower leaves gradually fall as the trunk grows. It can be bred by planting sprouts from the parent plant.

Sedum brevifolium

Spring-Fall | **8 cm**

It has dainty leaves covered with white powder. Its appealing form makes it a good accent plant for mixed arrangements.

Sedum burrito

Spring-Fall | **8 cm**

The thick, fleshy, bumpy leaves grow in a way that ultimately give them a burgeoning look. The shape makes it a work well in mixed arrangements.

Sedum *'Canny Hinny'*

Spring-Fall | **10 cm**

It grows rosettes of small leaves in clusters. The tips of the leaves turn pink during winter, giving it a pretty air.

Sedum clavatum

Spring-Fall | **8 cm**

The rosettes have thick oval leaves that lend a strong presence. It works well as the main role in sedum arrangements.

Sedum dasyphyllum

Spring-Fall | **10 cm**

The base variant of Sedum dasyphyllum. It is the smallest member of the family. It is sensitive to high humidity and its leaves turn purple in winter.

Sedum dasyphyllum *'Major'*

Spring-Fall | **8 cm**

It has small, plump rosettes that grow in clusters. The stems stretch if the plant does not get enough sunlight.

Sedum dasyphyllum var. glanduliferum

Spring-Fall **8 cm**

A larger variety of Sedum dasyphyllum (p. 79). The leaves turn purple when exposed to cold.

Sedum dendroideum

Spring-Fall **8 cm**

Unique shape that looks rather like a dancer in festive costume. The leaves turn reddish purple during winter. It is prone to growing too long when it lacks sunlight.

Sedum 'Dream Star'

Spring-Fall **10 cm**

A very tough variety that tolerates drought and does not wither even when hit by snow or frost. This plant makes excellent groundcover.

Sedum furfuraceum

Spring-Fall **7 cm**

Its stems are woody and short so this plant can be enjoyed as a bonsai as well. The round leaves are covered in scaly white granules.

Sedum glaucophyllum

Spring-Fall **10 cm**

Has stylish rosettes with shorter leaves on the inside that stretch outward. It works well as the main plant in mixed arrangements.

Sedum hakonense

Spring-Fall **10 cm**

It's native to the area around Hakone in Kanto, Japan. It is resistant to rain and should be grown separately from other succulents.

Sedum hernandezii

Spring-Fall **10 cm**

Its unique foliage is easily recognized at a glance. It is prone to stretching when it lacks sunlight or has been watered excessively.

Sedum hintonii

Spring-Fall **7 cm**

It looks very similar to Sedum mocinianum but has longer flower stalks. The leaves are covered in fine white spikes.

Sedum hispanicum purpurea

Spring-Fall **10 cm**

Its leaves keep a beautiful grayish purple color year round. It can be bred by planting its sprouts or separating the parents and the offspring when replanting.

Sedum 'Koigokoro'

Spring-Fall   **8 cm**

It looks like an enlarged Sedum pachyphyllum. It grows upward, so it needs to be trimmed regularly.

Sedum lineare f. variegata

Spring-Fall   **10 cm**

It's a speckled variant of Sedum lineare. Native to Japan and easy to grow.

Sedum lucidum

Spring-Fall   **10 cm**

It has glossy typical sedum leaves. It grows upward and produces multiple flowers at the tip of the flower stalks.

Sedum mexicanum

Spring-Fall   **10 cm**

A common plant found on roadsides in many parts of the world. It grows flower stalks and yellow flowers in spring.

Sedum pachyphyllum

Spring-Fall   **8 cm**

A variety characterized by the red color at the tips of its leaves. The color becomes brighter when kept in full sun and with moderate fertilizer and watering.

Sedum pallidum

Spring-Fall   **10 cm**

It grows white flowers in early summer and its leaves turn red in winter. It also grows a multitude of yellow flowers, giving its Japanese nickname "Pearl Star."

Sedum palmeri

Spring-Fall   **11 cm**

Its lime green leaves turn pink in winter and later turn a bright, flower petal-like red.

Sedum reflexum 'Chameleon' f. variegata

Spring-Fall   **8 cm**

The off-white dots turn to a pale azure color in winter. It works well as an accent plant in mixed arrangements.

Sedum 'Rotty'

Spring-Fall   **8 cm**

Grows smooth, glossy rosettes that work well as the main subject in mixed arrangements. Its shape makes it look cozy in the pot.

Sedum rubens

Spring-Fall **8 cm**

Rather than growing upward, it grows horizontally, giving it a bit of "dangle" that adds to arrangements. The red stems are a nice accent in group plantings.

Sedum rubrotinctum

Spring-Fall **10 cm**

The green-to-scarlet bean-like leaves really stand out. Bright sunlight maximizes the color potential. A stunning accent in mixed arrangements.

Sedum rupestre 'Angelina'

Spring-Fall **10 cm**

It has orange foliage in winter. It's resistant to cold and can be used as a groundcover plant. It grows yellow flowers in summer.

Sedum spurium 'Dragon's Blood'

Spring-Fall **10 cm**

Although its leaves fall off and only the stems survive the winter, the plants are still alive and regrow leaves in spring.

Sedum spurium 'Tricolor'

Spring-Fall **10 cm**

Has green, white, and pink leaves. Together with 'Dragon's Blood' it works great as an accent plant in mixed arrangements.

Sedum stahlii

Spring-Fall **8 cm**

A hybrid of rubrotinctum. Its dark red leaves turn either green or light red depending on the season and its environment.

Sedum stefco

Spring-Fall **10 cm**

It grows in clusters with fine leaves. Its leaves turn bright red in winter. A good standalone plant, as it likes to overflow from its pot.

Sedum treleasei

Spring-Fall **10 cm**

A rounded, soft green plant. It grows upward, so it needs to be trimmed regularly. Does not tolerate high temperatures and humidity.

Sedum versadense f. chontalense

Spring-Fall **8 cm**

It has thick, small leaves. In colder months, the underside of the leaves look like red valentine hearts.

Sedeveria
Crassulaceae genus

Place of Origin: None (hybrid)
Growth Difficulty: 3/3
Type: Spring-Fall, Summer
Watering: When the soil dries out, water generously. Mostly stop watering during summer and winter.

Characteristics They are an intergeneric hybrid of Sedum and Echeveria. They have a combination of characteristics from both families: the toughness and strength of Sedum is combined with much of the form of the lovely but harder-to-grow Echeveria. The resulting plants are easy to grow and maintain.

Tips for Cultivation Basically the same as sedums. Just like sedums, they like having full sunlight, but avoid direct sunlight in midsummer.

Sedeveria *'Blue Mist'*

A hybrid between Sedum craigii and Echeveria affinis. It has a beautiful purple hue that changes over the seasons.

Spring-Fall | 8 cm

Sedeveria *'Jet Beads'*

Spring-Fall | 8 cm

It's bright green in summer and turns a deep, glossy reddish brown in colder months. It's a variety with very enjoyable color changes.

Sedeveria *'Darley Dale'*

It grows a rosette with a large flower-like shape in the middle. It works well as the main plant in a mixed arrangement. It grows cream-colored star-shaped flowers.

Spring-Fall | 8 cm

Spring-Fall **9 cm**

There's a beautiful contrast between green and red leaves in winter. Move indoors when temperatures drop below 32°F/0°C.

Spring-Fall **8 cm**

It has muscat green leaves with saturated pink edges. Grows in large clusters with short stems.

Sedeveria *'Rolly'*

Sedeveria *'Seiya-tsuzuri'*

Sedeveria *'Whitestone Crop'*

Spring-Fall **12 cm**

Grows a trunk with offspring growing on the lower part, giving the plant a very compact appearance. It's susceptible to high humidity.

Spring-Fall **10 cm**

A hybrid between Echeveria derenbergii (p.48) and Sedum tamatsuzuri. The tips of the leaves turn orange in winter.

Spring-Fall **8 cm**

It grows in small rosettes (about ¾"/2cm in size) with pink to red leaves. It makes a good accent in mixed arrangements.

Obtaining Succulents: Cutting off growing stems or branches and re-tailoring

(PETIT)

Pachyphytum rzedowskii

Spring-Fall

Its color changes over the seasons. Susceptible to high humidity.

1 Cut off the stretched part.

2 The stems have been cut.

3 Remove the leaves so that about ⅜"/1cm of stem is left. Let the cut ends dry.

4 When the roots emerge, plant in dry culture medium soil.

Pachyphytum
Crassulaceae genus

Place of Origin: Mexico
Growth Difficulty: 2/3
Type: Spring-Fall
Watering: Water generously when the soil dries out. Reduce watering during winter and Summer to about once a month.

Characteristics The leaves are characterized by their plump, round shape the fine white powder covering them. The white powder will come off if touched, so when repotting, hold the lower part of their stems only.

Tips for Cultivation Keep them in a sunny and well-ventilated place. If they lack sunlight they start to stretch and lose color. They should be repotted every year or two.

Pachyphytum compactum

The white streaks that appear on its leaves during growth are characteristic of this variety. In colder months, the leaves turn a yellow orange color. It's similar to Pachyphytum glaucum, which has purple foliage during winter instead.

Spring-Fall **8 cm**

Pachyphytum *'Gekkabijin'* f. variegata

The rosette created by its spreading spatula-like leaves is gorgeous. It has a strong presence and works well as the main plant in mixed arrangements

Spring-Fall **10 cm**

Pachyphytum hookeri

It grows upward on a trunk like a tree. The pointed white tip on each leaf is its main feature.

Spring-Fall **10 cm**

Pachyphytum oviferum *'Hoshibijin'*

One of the many Pachyphytum species that contain "beautiful woman" in their Japanese nickname. The light purple foliage covered with white powder gives a graceful impression.

Spring-Fall **8 cm**

Sempervivum
Crassulaceae genus

Place of Origin: Highlands in Central-South Europe
Growth Difficulty: 2/3
Type: Spring-Fall
Watering: Water generously when the soil dries out. Reduce watering during winter and Summer. Almost stop watering altogether in summer, especially.

Characteristics They have beautiful foliage with multiple layers of fine leaves arranged in rosette shapes. Their leaves turn red in winter. They have been very popular in Europe for a long time, and there are many garden varieties in various colors and shapes. Its scientific name comes from Latin and means "ever alive."

Tips for Cultivation They are native to the harsh environments of the mountainous regions in Europe. They are quite resistant to cold weather and low humidity, which allows them to be cultivated outdoors all year long depending on your area. They are however susceptible to high humidity at high temperatures and should be moved to well-ventilated places in half-shade during the rainy season and summer.

Sempervivum *'Fusiller'*

It has leaves with fine hairs on the edges. The thin, spiky leaves, its coloring, and the runners give it a wild atmosphere.

Spring-Fall   **11 cm**

Sempervivum *'Marine'*

Its color changes to an attractive dark purple in winter. It grows plenty of offspring in clusters. Works well as the main subject in chic mixed arrangements.

Spring-Fall   **8 cm**

Sempervivum *'Oddity'*

Its leaves curl up into a characteristic cylindrical shape. Water the soil surrounding the plant so that water doesn't collect on the leaves.

Spring-Fall   **11 cm**

Sempervivum *'Pacific Knight'*

It has beautiful colors that change from green to wine depending on the season. It produces runners and plenty of offspring.

Spring-Fall   **11 cm**

Sempervivum 'Rose-Marie'

Its tight rosettes and deep wine color are very typical of sempervivum. It makes a good accent for mixed arrangements.

Spring-Fall **11 cm**

Sempervivum 'Shanghai Rose'

A variety with a very graceful appearance. The purple of the edges becomes denser in the center. It produces plenty of offspring.

Spring-Fall **8 cm**

Sempervivum 'Strawberry Velvet'

Its leaves are covered with delicate hairs giving them a velvety appearance. It has beautiful seasonal coloring.

Spring-Fall **11 cm**

Sempervivum tectorum 'Koukunka '

It has large rose-like rosettes. It can be enjoyed both on its own, or as the main plant in a mixed arrangement.

Spring-Fall **8 cm**

Obtaining Succulents: Cutting off growing stems or branches and re-tailoring

PETIT

Sempervivum 'Marine'

1 The pot is getting full.

2 The roots are very thin, so break the soil up carefully.

3 While loosening the roots, separate the offspring.

4 Also remove withered leaves.

5 The parent and offspring are now divided.

6 The parent and the offspring have been planted separately.

Tylecodon
Crassulaceae genus

Place of Origin: Southern Africa
Growth Difficulty: 2/3
Type: Winter **Watering:** Water generously when the soil dries out. Reduce watering during the rainy season. Almost no watering at all in summer.

Characteristics A representative winter type genus of caudex. They lose its leaves in summer, with new leaves emerging again when temperatures drop in fall. They mainly grow flowers in spring. There is a wide variety of them, from small varieties only a few cm in length to large species that grow over 39"/1m in height.

Tips for Cultivation In summer, the plant goes into dormancy so keep it in a well-ventilated place with little water and plenty of shade. In fall, when new leaves start to appear, begin watering gradually. In spring and fall, water generously when the soil is completely dry. Water a little less in winter.

Tylecodon paniculatus

This variety is characterized by its thin, papery skin that covers the thick trunk full of water. Its characteristics are a clear result of having evolved to resist habitats with very few nutrients.

Winter **12 cm**

Tylecodon reticulatus

The thin, branch-like growths around the leaves are actually hardened flower peduncles left behind after flowering. Its growth is very slow.

Winter **13 cm**

Hylotelephium cauticola

Spring-Fall **11 cm**

A variety that is native to Hokkaido. The egg-shaped leaves are about ¾"/2cm in size and covered with white powder. The leaves turn red in fall.

Hylotelephium
Crassulaceae genus

Place of Origin: Asia **Growth Difficulty:** 3/3
Type: Spring-Fall **Watering:** Water generously when the soil dries out. Slightly reduce frequency in winter.

Characteristics
They are a tough herb-like genus that grows mainly in mountainous areas, rocky areas in valleys, and on cliffs near coasts. In fall, they grow flowers and their leaves turn red. In winter, they lose their leaves and go into dormancy, but grow again in spring.

Tips for Cultivation
They enjoy being in a sunny and well-ventilated places. They are quite resistant to cold weather and can be grown outdoors over the winter in many regions. As they are susceptible to high humidity, keep them properly covered during rainy periods and make sure no water gets on their leaves. Can be bred by dividing offspring, and replanting or by planting their seedlings.

Rosularia

Crassulaceae genus

Place of Origin: From Northern Africa to Central Asia
Growth Difficulty: 2/3
Type: Spring-Fall **Watering:** Water generously when the soil dries out. Reduce watering during winter and summer, bringing watering almost to a stop in summer.

Characteristics

They are close relatives to Sempervivum. The leaves are arranged in multiple rosettes, and offspring grows in clusters around the parent plants. The difference is that the leaves of Sempervivum are divided, while Rosularia leaves are tubular.

Tips for Cultivation

Almost the same as Sempervivum. They are tough and resistant to both heat and cold, but are susceptible to direct sunlight and humidity in midsummer. During the growing season, water generously when the soil dries out.

Rosularia chrysantha

It has rosettes of small, thick leaves covered with fine hairs that grow in clusters.

Spring-Fall	8 cm

Rosularia platyphylla

It grows plenty of offspring. Keep it exposed to full sunlight to grow in a nice, tight shape.

Spring-Fall	7 cm

Monanthes

Crassulaceae genus

Place of Origin: Canary Island, etc. **Growth Difficulty:** 1/3
Type: Spring-Fall **Watering:** Water generously when the soil dries out. Reduce watering during summer to about once a month.

Characteristics

A very small family with small, fleshy leaves that grow in tight clusters. They grow naturally in shady, moist, rocky areas. The temperature in their native habitat doesn't vary much throughout the year, ranging with temperatures from 59–80°F/15–27 °C with little to no rainfall. So, they are very susceptible to excessive cold, heat and humidity.

Tips for Cultivation

Keep in well-ventilated half-shade places. Susceptibility to heat and humidity can make them wither and melt altogether in summer. When temperatures exceed 95°F/35°C, it is safer to keep them indoors in front of a sunny window during the daytime.

Monanthes polyphylla

Spring-Fall	8 cm

The attractive rosettes are made of many small leaves and are just under an inch (about 2cm) in diameter. It also grows unusual-looking purple or orange flowers.

Aloe

Crassulaceae genus

Place of Origin: Southern Africa, Madagascar, Arabian Peninsula, etc.

Growth Difficulty: 3/3

Type: Summer **Watering:** Water generously when the soil dries out. Reduce watering during winter .

Characteristics A large genus made of over 700 species, ranging from small species to large trees that grow more than 33'/10m in height. There are many popular varieties: Aloe arborescens is well-known as a medicinal plant, and aloe vera is a well-known edible variety; but there is also a wide variety of garden species that are fun to grow.

Tips for Cultivation Aloe vera is strong, resistant to summer heat, and easy to grow, but growing tips vary from variety to variety. When they lack sufficient sunlight, they may stretch, so keep them under good sunlight at all times. Some species can be grown outdoors in winter bit in colder regions, it is safer to move them indoors in front of a bright window.

Aloe aculeata var. Limpopo

It grows stiff, horn-like leaves that alternate from side to side and turn reddish purple in fall.

Summer	8 cm

Aloe albiflora

It grows white bell-shaped flowers, which are unusual in the Aloe family. It also has no stems, and its slender leaves have white spots and thorns on them.

Summer	11 cm

Aloe aristata 'Ouhi-ayanishiki'

A popular variety because of the green to red gradation of its broad leaves and its well-defined rosette shape.

Summer	13 cm

Aloe 'Blizzard'

The large, dynamic-looking leaves with their blizzard-like white spot pattern make this a good summer plant.

Summer	16 cm

Aloe capitata

It is characterized by its red thorns and edges. It is native to Madagascar, where several varieties of this plant can be found.

Summer | **9 cm**

Aloe *'Dapple Green'*

A beautiful variety with fine white speckles. In winter, it grows flower stalks that blossom with pretty bell-shaped flowers.

Summer | **16 cm**

Aloe dichotoma

In its native habitat, it can grow to a height of 33'/10m or more. It grows in a small size if cultivated in small pots. Its roots are delicate so it requires special care when replanting.

Summer | **13 cm**

Aloe ferox

Its leaves grow in a ring that goes around their trunk-like stem, with dynamic reddish-brown spikes. It grows as a single tree without branching.

Summer | **15 cm**

Aloe *'Fire Bird'*

It branches a lot and creates many clusters. When the long flower stalks bloom they give the plant a bonsai-like appearance.

Summer | **16 cm**

Aloe *'Flamingo'*

Characterized by its bright red spikes. The name 'Flamingo' is derived from the Latin for "flame" (*flamma*), referring to red color of flames rather than the pink of the popular bird.

Summer | **12 cm**

Summer · **16 cm**

A small variant growing in clusters. The spines on the entire leaf are not sharp/painful. Its leaves turn orange during colder months.

Summer · **14 cm**

The trunks grow upward like towers. The glossy jade green leaves turn light orange in winter.

Summer · **16 cm**

A vigorous, prolific growing variety, with the trunk growing upward. It needs to be trimmed regularly.

Aloe *'Pink Blush'*

Summer · **16 cm**

Its color becomes darker in colder months. It grows long flower stalks in fall that blossom into pink to yellow flowers.

Aloe ramosissima

Summer · **17 cm**

It has characteristically narrow, upturned leaves. It divides into new branches easily and cultivating it into a nice shape can be very fun.

Aloe rauhii *'White Fox'*

Summer · **15 cm**

It has a beautiful, speckled pattern on its grayish leaves. The long flower stalks are well balanced.

Obtaining Succulents: There are plenty of offspring sprouts and the pot is getting cramped

PETIT

Aloe rauhii *'White Fox'*

1 Remove the plant from the pot.

2 Break up and remove the soil with your fingers.

3 Gently separate the offspring, taking care of not damaging the roots.

4 Cut off the withered roots with scissors.

5 The parent and offspring have been separated.

6 1 month after planting the parent and the offspring, they are starting to flower.

Astroloba
Asphodelaceae genus

Place of Origin: Southern Africa
Growth Difficulty: 3/3
Type: Spring-Fall **Watering:** From spring to fall, water generously when the soil dries out. Reduce watering during summer and winter.

Characteristics
The 'astro' in the name is derived by the fact that their leaves look like stars when viewed from above. They grow in wild trunks reaching upward similarly to Haworthia. Their growth pattern is also similar to Haworthia.

Tips for Cultivation
Grow in half-shade and keep in well-ventilated places. Keep in half-shade all year long as they do not tolerate direct sunlight. In spring and fall, water the plants generously when the soil dries out, but during their dormant periods in summer and winter, only water moderately and let the plants dry out between waterings.

Astroloba skinneri

`Spring-Fall`　`8 cm`

This popular variety has leaves that soar upward in a radial shape. The papillae on the leaves give it a rough and interesting texture.

Astroloba sp.

`Spring-Fall`　`8 cm`

The Japanese name for this plant translates as "Ursa Minor." Its chubby leaves are piled on top of each other. As they are very weak to leaf burn, use shade nets or other measures to protect it from direct sunlight.

Kumara
Asphodelaceae genus

Place of Origin: Southern Africa **Growth Difficulty:** 3/3
Type: Spring-Fall **Watering:** From spring to fall, water generously when the soil dries out. Reduce watering during winter.

Characteristics
They were considered members of the aloe family until 2014, but have recently been redefined. The stem grows upward and the trunk becomes woody, with some species reaching up to 16'/5m in height.

Tips for Cultivation
As with other species in the genus Aloe, grow them in well-ventilated, sunny environments. Water generously when the soil dries out and allow the soil to dry out before watering again. In winter, watering should be only moderate and the plant should be kept indoors in full sun.

Kumara plicatilis

`Spring-Fall`　`15 cm`

It has a really beautiful form. It is sensitive to cold, so when the temperatures drop below 59°F/15°C, move indoors in full sun.

Gasteria

Asphodelaceae genus

Place of Origin: Southern Africa
Growth Difficulty: 3/3
Type: Summer type but close to Spring-Fall type
Watering: From spring to fall, water generously when the soil dries out. Reduce watering during winter.

Characteristics Their tongue-shaped leaves (with rounded or pointed tips) spread symmetrically. The genus name means "stomach" in Latin and derives from the shape of the flowers.

Tips for Cultivation Although they are summer types, they are susceptible high to midsummer heat, so keep them in a well-ventilated spot in half-shade or use shade nets to avoid direct sunlight. Move them indoors during winter when the temperature drops below 41°F/5°C.

Gasteria armstrongii

Summer | **9 cm**

It has symmetrical leaves that alternate from side to side and overlap densely. It does not tolerate direct sunlight and is prone to leaf bean so take care of them.

Gasteria baylissiana

Summer | **8 cm**

It has distinctive white spots and fringes on its leaves. It grows plenty of offspring in clusters.

Gasteria 'Flow'

Summer | **9 cm**

The sword-like leaves are arranged radially, giving it a sharp image. Relatively easy to grow, it makes a good houseplant.

Gasteria glomerata

Summer | **8 cm**

It has characteristic thick, whitish leaves. The leaves are easily damaged by humidity, causing spots to appear on the surface, so take extra care.

Gasteria gracilis var. minima f. variegata

Summer | **8 cm**

The tongue-shaped leaves are stacked like cards and spread out like a fan. It produces many seedlings and grows in clusters.

Gasteria 'Little Warty'

Summer **9 cm**

It has a unique leaf shape with lines, dots, and many colors of green on a single leaf.

Gasteria pillansii 'Kyoryu' f. variegata

Summer **12 cm**

Creates a unique form with wide, stiff leaves that alternate from side to side. It grows slowly.

Gasteria pulchra

Summer **8 cm**

It's unique in that its narrow leaves turn in many different direction, as if they're dancing. It grows in small clusters.

PETIT

Obtaining Succulents: There are plenty of offspring sprouts and the pot is getting cramped

Gasteria baillisiana
This is a small succulent plant with a large number of young plants and a dense root system.

1 Break off the soil with your fingers.

2 Holding the base of the parent plant tightly makes the offspring easier to remove.

3 Clean the roots and separate the plants.

4 One month later, the parent plant is already growing new offspring.

Gasteraloe
Asphodelaceae genus

Place of Origin: None (hybrid) **Growth Difficulty:** 3/3
Type: Summer **Watering:** Water generously when the soil dries out. Reduce watering during winter.

Characteristics & Tips for Cultivation
An intergeneric hybrid of Gasteria and Aloe. The flowers are similar to those of aloe, and new sprouts grow in clusters. In general, you want to follow the same cultivation methods as Gasteria. They are strong and easy to grow. Keep in a well-ventilated place and exposed to full sunlight except for direct sunlight in midsummer.

Gasteraloe 'Green Ice'

Spring-Fall **10 cm**

The pattern of dots differs from one variant to another. The plant produces tubular flowers that variegate from blush/red at the base to green at the tip.

Haworthia

Asphodelaceae genus

Place of Origin: Southern Africa
Growth Difficulty: 2/3
Type: Spring-Fall **Watering:** From spring to fall, water generously when the soil dries out. Reduce watering during its dormancy period in summer and in winter.

Characteristics In their native habitat, they live quietly behind rocks, at the base of trees, or protected by weeds. There are several types of Haworthia: soft types with beautiful transparent "windows," tough types with stiff leaves, lacy types with white hairs on their leaves, and others with the top part cut off horizontally.

Tips for Cultivation Most Haworthias are sensitive to direct sunlight, so they should be grown in half-shade and well-ventilated spots. During the spring and fall growing season, water generously when the soil in the pot dries out and prevent the soil from becoming too dry. In winter, keep them in temperatures above 41°F/5°C.

Haworthia 'Akanko'

Spring-Fall   11 cm

It has beautiful deep green large leaves with a linear pattern that directs light into its "window." The leaves will grow long and thin if it does not get enough sunlight.

Haworthia arachnoidea

Spring-Fall   8 cm

It's a representative species of lacy Haworthia, and there are many variations. It is characterized by its translucent spines

Haworthia attenuate

Spring-Fall   8 cm

The beautiful pattern on the leaves looks like snow. In colder months, the white snow pattern changes to a light vermilion color.

Haworthia 'Audeley'

Spring-Fall   11 cm

The long flower stalks are one of the main characteristics of Haworthia. Letting all of its flowers bloom weakens the plant. So cut some of the flower stems before they blossom, leaving just over an inch (about 3cm) of stem (pull out the stems when they are completely withered).

Haworthia coarctata

Spring-Fall · **9 cm**

Similar to the reinwardtii variety, but the white pattern is smaller and tends to a thin, linear pattern.

Haworthia coarctata *'Baccata'*

Spring-Fall · **8 cm**

Grows on a thick trunk with overlapping leaves. It grows offspring in clusters. It's also susceptible to direct sunlight.

Haworthia *'Black Shark'*

Spring-Fall · **8 cm**

The window at the tip of the leaf has a unique shape not found on other Haworthia plants. It also has small protuberances.

Haworthia *'Chinadress'*

Spring-Fall · **8 cm**

The narrow leaves are dotted and the whole plant looks beautifully translucent. The edge of the leaves have short, thin serrations.

Haworthia cooperi *'Akasen Lens'*

Spring-Fall · **8 cm**

The leaves are slightly reddish. It has impressive transparent windows.

Haworthia cooperi hyb. glowing obtusa

Spring-Fall · **8 cm**

With a lamé-like pattern courtesy of its hybrid parent, Haworthia turgida var. pallidifolia (p.107), it has yellow-green transparent windows.

Haworthia cooperi hyb Daruma cooperi

Spring-Fall · **9 cm**

A variant characterized by reddish leaves with a large round window on the leaf tip.

Haworthia cooperi hyb. green obtusa

Spring-Fall · **8 cm**

The window is also yellowish green, giving the whole plant a strong green look.

Haworthia cooperi hyb. white-skin obtusa

Spring-Fall · **8 cm**

More matte and whitish variant of Haworthia truncata (p. 98).

Haworthia cooperi hyb. Tenshin obtusa

Spring-Fall **8 cm**

Has slightly purple leaves.

Haworthia cooperi var. leightonii 'Ryokuin'

Spring-Fall **8 cm**

A variant of leightonii with short hairs at the tips of spiky leaves. As shown here, these relatively vertical leaves can be intensely red as well as green.

Haworthia cooperi var. leightonii 'Shiden'

Spring-Fall **8 cm**

It has dark green leaves with short hairs on the spiky tips, a typical characteristic of the leightonii species.

Haworthia cooperi var. pilifera

Spring-Fall **8 cm**

It has vertical, crystalline leaves. It rarely grows from leaves, so offspring separation is the best way to breed them.

Haworthia cooperi var. pilifera f. variegata

Spring-Fall **8 cm**

A popular variety with beautiful transparent white spots. It's weak to strong light, so it should be placed in bright half-shade instead.

Haworthia cooperi var. truncata

Spring-Fall **8 cm**

A very typical soft-leaved Haworthia. The small, rounded leaves grow in dense clusters.

Classification of Haworthia types (1)

NOTE

Haworthia with translucent leaf tips that sparkle beautifully when held against the light are referred to as "soft-leaved type," also called "obtusa-type."

The "window" on their leaves evolved in Haworthia's native South African habitat—where the plant grows half-buried in arid soil or hidden behind rocks—to let in light.

Haworthia can be classified in two different ways. One sorts them into "obtusa-type" or "lace-type." The second classification (presented in p.108) divides them between retusa, truncata and pumila families.

Obtusa
Haworthia with a "window" at the tip of the leaf to let in light.

Haworthia 'Tamaazusa'

Lace-type
Slender, spiny or serrated leaves characterize this type.

Arachnoidea

Haworthia cuspidata

Spring-Fall | **9 cm**

The wide, thick-walled leaves form star-shaped rosettes. Replant regularly as it grows offspring often.

Haworthia cymbiformis var. angustata

Spring-Fall | **11 cm**

The shape of the rosettes look like rose flowers. The tips of the leaves turn pink in colder months.

Haworthia 'Dragon Ball'

Spring-Fall | **8 cm**

It grows in a dense rosette of plump leaves. The emerging offspring are also thick. Weak to heat and high humidity.

Haworthia emelyae

Spring-Fall | **13 cm**

This plant grows in a single cluster of fleshy rosettes. The triangular leaf tips have a rough and uneven shape. It has several varieties.

Haworthia emelyae var. major

Spring-Fall | **8 cm**

The windows are covered with thick, short, hair-like protuberances, giving it a rugged appearance.

Haworthia fasciata 'Choveriba'

Spring-Fall | **8 cm**

Haworthia fasciata are also known as the Zebra Plant due to the wide horizontal bands that give it such a pronounced striped pattern. The inside of the leaves are monochromatic and smooth.

Haworthia fasciata 'Hakucho'

Spring-Fall | **8 cm**

A dotted variety of 'Jyuni-no-maki'. The lime green leaves give a fresh look.

Haworthia fasciata 'Jyuni-no-maki'

Spring-Fall | **9 cm**

The most common variety of Haworthia fasciata. The outside part of its leaves has a stripe pattern of connected white dots.

Haworthia fasciata 'Jyuni-no-tsume'

Spring-Fall | **8 cm**

Its leaves bend gently inward and have a red tip that looks rather like a fingernail.

Haworthia fasciata *'Short Leaf'*

Spring-Fall | **8 cm**

It has narrower and shorter leaves than other Haworthia. Its white dots are connected along the leaf edges.

Haworthia fasciata *'Super Wide Band'*

Spring-Fall | **8 cm**

It's yet another variant of 'Jyuni-no-tsume' but is a striking species nonetheless with its thick white stripes.

Haworthia *'Gamera'*

Spring-Fall | **9 cm**

A beautiful hybrid derived from bolusii, with sharp edges that give this plant a claw-like appearance.

Haworthia glauca var. herrei

Spring-Fall | **8 cm**

It has sword-like leaves vary in shade of green and are textured with ridges and bumps. It often produces offspring that grows in clusters.

Haworthia gracilis

Spring-Fall | **10 cm**

The rosette looks like a flower blooming. It often grows new sprouts in clusters, so it should be trimmed regularly.

Haworthia gracilis var. picturata

Spring-Fall | **9 cm**

A variant of Haworthia gracilis. It has beautiful light yellow-green translucent windows. Careful of direct sunlight and high humidity.

Haworthia *'Green Gem'*

Spring-Fall | **8 cm**

An unusual shape among Haworthia hybrids. Its hybrid parents are maughanii and truncata (p.98).

Haworthia *'Green Rose'*

Spring-Fall | **8 cm**

A cross between a retusa and a truncata, which grows into a rose-like flower shape. It is truly a wonder of crossbreeding.

Haworthia *'Hakuteijyo'*

Spring-Fall | **9 cm**

A favorite of many because of its crystal-like coloration. The windows are covered in translucent dots.

Haworthia hyb. Correcta x Spring

Spring-Fall **10 cm**

The chic-colored windows have intricate line patterns. The family previously called collecta is now called picta.

Haworthia hyb. 'Snow White Emaki'

Spring-Fall **8 cm**

A hybrid of Echeveria 'Shirayukihime' (p.58) and Haworthia cooperi var. venusta. Characterized by soft, thin, linear protuberances.

Haworthia hyb. Shunrai x Aurora

Spring-Fall **10 cm**

The pattern on the window is inherited from Aurora. The transparency of the window is similar to that of Shunrai.

Haworthia 'Koteki'

Spring-Fall **8 cm**

It grows short triangular leaves with fine white dots on the outside. It often produces offspring that grow in clusters.

Haworthia 'Koteki Nishiki'

Spring-Fall **8 cm**

A speckled species of Haworthia 'Koteki Nishiki'. Yellow-green and cream-colored spots are distributed randomly over the leaves. It can be used to add color to mixed arrangements.

Haworthia limifolia

Spring-Fall **8 cm**

It has wide overlapping leaves growing in many directions. It's the original variant of the limifolia family. It is characterized by the ridges that give the leaves a raised stripe look and feel.

Haworthia limifolia f. variegata

Spring-Fall **11 cm**

It is a variety of limifolia with yellow spots. The irregularity of the markings on the leaves makes each individual plant truly unique.

Haworthia limiforia 'Striata'

Spring-Fall **9 cm**

The density of the ridges on this variety can make the plant seem almost white. While the plant remains short, the flower stalk can grow over 12"/30cm tall.

Haworthia magnifica sp.

Spring-Fall **8 cm**

A variant of magnifica with triangular windows that open wide. It has many other variants and is often used in hybrids.

Haworthia 'Manda's hybrid'

Spring-Fall **8 cm**

Its main characteristic is its bright lime-green leaves. It often produces offspring that grow in clusters.

Haworthia 'Manteri'

Spring-Fall **8 cm**

Characterized by its crystal-like shape. A hybrid of cooperi and maughanii.

Haworthia maughanii 'Daimonji'

Spring-Fall **8 cm**

It has dark green leaves with a distinct white line pattern. It is a variety that has many fans but is rather rare.

Haworthia maughanii 'Shiko'

Spring-Fall **10 cm**

It has purplish green leaves. The pattern of the lines on the window is not white, but instead a light greenish color.

Haworthia maughanii 'Hyosetsu'

Spring-Fall **10 cm**

The leaves spread out in a shape that looks like a fan, but it is classified as part of the maughanii family. The pattern on the window looks like snowflakes.

Haworthia maughanii 'Yukiguni'

Spring-Fall **8 cm**

It has a translucent white window with a pattern of small lines. The color of the leaves is also semitransparent and elegant.

Haworthia 'Miller Ball'

Spring-Fall **8 cm**

It has large, glossy windows and short, thin serrations at the tips of the leaves. A popular variety of the cooperi hybrids.

Haworthia mirabilis var. mundla

Spring-Fall **8 cm**

One of the many varieties of Haworthia mirabilis. It has short leaves with a simple yellow-green line in the window.

Haworthia mirabilis var. paradoxa

Spring-Fall **8 cm**

The surface of its leaves is covered with transparent dots.

Haworthia 'Ollasonii'

Spring-Fall **8 cm**

The brownish leaves and the greenish windows create interesting contrast. Works well as the main plant in Haworthia arrangements.

Haworthia picta

Spring-Fall **8 cm**

The small white spots in the window look deep green from some angles. The picta also has many varieties and hybrids.

Haworthia picta 'Cleopatra x Mevius'

Spring-Fall **10 cm**

The white spots on the rounded, plump window give an elegant impression.

Haworthia 'Princess Dress'

Spring-Fall **9 cm**

It has sleek leaves and large windows. An elegant hybrid with semi-translucent parts. In spring, it grows flower stalks and blooms white flowers.

Haworthia pumila × 'Baccata'

Spring-Fall **8 cm**

This is a mysterious hybrid between two members of the pumila family with a cute look. The leaves are tight and well-shaped.

Haworthia pumila 'Papillosa'

Spring-Fall **8 cm**

The dark green, thick leaves have a lovely icing-like cover of small circles. It is tough and easy to grow.

Haworthia pygmaea

Spring-Fall **9 cm**

The tops of the leaves appear faintly white because they are covered in short white hairs.

Haworthia pygmaea 'Super White'

Spring-Fall **10 cm**

It has white protuberances growing in a single linear pattern. The windows are round and raised, and the entire plant is pretty round.

Haworthia reinwardtii

Spring-Fall **8 cm**

A tight variety with white dots all over. The plants often produce offspring that grow in clusters at the base of the parent plant.

Haworthia reinwardtii 'Kaffirdriftensis'

Spring-Fall | **9 cm**

Most species with white dots have them arranged around the borders, but Kaffirdriffensis has them vertically aligned.

Haworthia reinwardtii var. archibaldiae

Spring-Fall | **8 cm**

Each leaf has a rounded backside and is dotted with white nodules, a pattern that makes this plant look like a forest of stars.

Haworthia resendeana

Spring-Fall | **8 cm**

It grows in a beautiful, three-leafed rotating pattern that extends upward. It also looks great when it's growing in clusters.

Haworthia reticulata

Spring-Fall | **8 cm**

Pale yellow-green leaves with translucent round spots. The polka dot look gives it a pretty atmosphere.

Haworthia retusa

Spring-Fall | **8 cm**

Haworthia retusa is characterized by its curved leaf tips and large, transparent, triangular windows. There are many varieties and hybrids.

Haworthia retusa hyb.

Spring-Fall | **8 cm**

A small retusa with faint yellowish-green spots. Prolific offspring and grows in clumps.

Obtaining Succulents: There are plenty of offspring sprouts and the pot is getting cramped

PETIT

Haworthia retusa

1 If the old roots are tangled or stuck with soil, gently free them with tweezers.

2 If the offspring roots are difficult to separate, try to remove them by poking them gently with tweezers and pulling.

3 If you still can't separate them, it's also okay to snap the roots off. Even if the roots of the seedlings are cut off, if you leave them on their own for a little while, new roots will eventually emerge.

4 Plant the parent and offspring separately to finish.

Haworthia mutica hyb.

Spring-Fall | **8 cm**

It has large, plump leaves which have a white window with linear green veins.

Haworthia 'Seiko'

A hybrid of truncata and retusa families. The central leaves are arranged in a line, but the outer leaves instead wrap around the plant as they grow.

Spring-Fall | **8 cm**

Haworthia splendens hyb.

Spring-Fall | **10 cm**

It has numerous white spots and small translucent round spots mostly around the tips of the thick-walled leaves.

Haworthia springbokvlakensis

Spring-Fall | **8 cm**

The leaf tips are rounded and flattened, with a linear pattern over large windows. It's often used as a hybrid parent.

Haworthia springbokvlakensis hyb.

Spring-Fall | **8 cm**

It has deep purple leaves with dark green translucent windows. A striking-looking hybrid with a dark atmosphere.

Haworthia springbokvlakensis 'Kaptha'

Spring-Fall | **10 cm**

A hybrid derived from Haworthia spring-bokvlakensis . The tips of the recurved leaves are small and look similar to maughanii.

Haworthia 'Tamaazusa'

Spring-Fall | **8 cm**

It has beautiful transparent windows. It is probably a cooperi-related hybrid, but hybrid parents are unknown.

Haworthia tessellata var. parva

Spring-Fall | **8 cm**

It has small, warped triangular windows with vertical lines. There are also many varieties and hybrids of Haworthia tessellata.

Haworthia tortuosa

Spring-Fall **9 cm**

Sharp, overlapping, tower-like trunks with sharp leaves growing in a ring shape. The leaves are topped with fine protuberances.

Haworthia tortuosa f. variegata

Spring-Fall **8 cm**

The sharp leaves have a white speckled pattern. It's a spotted variant of tortuosa.

Haworthia truncata 'Byakurei'

Spring-Fall **10 cm**

It has pale white lines propagating like waves on its brown leaves.

Haworthia truncata 'Lime Green'

Spring-Fall **8 cm**

This is not a hybrid of two truncata, but a hybrid with another Haworthia variety. Has a distinct lime green color.

Haworthia truncata 'Shironagasu'

Spring-Fall **10 cm** Its large and sturdy form looks just like a whale. Its white pattern can also resemble a beard.

Haworthia 'Tukikage'

Spring-Fall **12 cm**

Its leaves and windows are wet, glossy, and transparent. The net-like pattern stands out against the dark green windows.

Haworthia turgida f. variegata

Spring-Fall **9 cm**

The leaves and the windows are elongated, and the entire plant is quite transparent. The tips of its leaves curl up and add a sense of movement.

Haworthia turgida 'Tamamidori'

Spring-Fall **8 cm**

The small, triangular leaves grow into small rosettes that resemble roses. It grows offspring in clusters.

Haworthia turgida var. pallidifolia

Spring-Fall **8 cm**

It has small pale yellow-green windows and sparkling white dots. It's a gentle-looking variety.

Haworthia umbraticola

Spring-Fall **12 cm**

Its small triangular leaves form many rosettes and grow in tight clusters.

Haworthia 'Tiger Pig'

Spring-Fall **8 cm**

A hybrid between Haworthia 'Pigmaea' and Haworthia 'Kegani'. The 'Kegani' is also a hybrid, so this variety is a mixture of many varieties.

Haworthia 'Yukigeshiki'

Spring-Fall **8 cm**

It has a beautiful and picturesque combination of white spots, translucent patterned windows, and green lines.

Haworthia sp. 'Shishikotobuki'

Spring-Fall **8 cm**

It has little Jagged serrations. A small Haworthia with a brave look.

Haworthia sp. 'Sugar Plum'

Spring-Fall **8 cm**

It has deep green leaves, with windows on the tip of the leaves in the same color, it's the typical look of a dark green Haworthia.

Haworthia sp. 'Cecilifolia'

Spring-Fall **8 cm**

It has translucent green leaves with a purple underside. It grows plenty of offspring in clusters.

Haworthia sp. 'Tsuru no Shiro'

Spring-Fall **8 cm**

It has yellow-green leaves with a hint of red on the tips. The thin leaves have small white nodules that give it a delicate impression.

Haworthia sp. 'Kakyou'

Spring-Fall **8 cm**

It has translucent, bright green leaves spreading outwards. It grows in clusters, forming pretty rosettes.

Retusa Family
They have large, triangular, upturned leaves with windows on their tips. The spots and line patterns in the window are variegated.

Haworthia picta

Truncata Family
They have translucent windows at the tips of leaves that look as if they have been cut off. The leaves grow in a fan shape when seen from the side. The spiral shaped varieties are called maughanii.

**Haworthia truncata 'Shironagasu';
Haworthia truncata 'Shikou'**

Pumila Family
They have spiky, stiff leaves with stripes or dots (ridges or nodes) on them.

**Limiforia, Haworthia fasciata
'Jyuni-no-maki'**

Bulbine
Asphodelaceae genus

Place of Origin: Southern Africa
Growth Difficulty: 2/3 **Type:** Winter **Watering:** Between fall and spring water once the soil is completely dry. During summer, water in short amounts a few times a month.

Characteristics & Tips for Cultivation
From fall to spring, grow them in a sunny and well-ventilated place. If they lack sufficient sunlight, the leaves will stretch, so make sure to expose them to plenty of sunlight. When they go dormant in summer and the leaves begin to wither, keep them in a cool environment away from rain. They may wither and die if exposed to too much moisture.

Bulbine margrethae

`Winter` `8 cm`

It has thin leaves with a reticulate pattern. The leaves turn purplish-red in winter. It grows thick tuberous roots in the soil.

Astroloba rubiflora (formerly Poellnitzia rubiflora)
Asphodelaceae genus

Place of Origin: Southern Africa
Growth Difficulty: 2/3 **Type:** Winter **Watering:** Between fall and spring water once the soil is completely dry. During summer, water in short amounts a few times a month.

Characteristics & Tips for Cultivation
A related family to Astroloba, with similar foliage (some say they should also be classified in the genus Astroloba). The tips for cultivation are basically the same as for Astroloba. Grow them in a semi-shady, well-ventilated environment.

Astroloba rubriflora

`Winter` `8 cm`

Originally placed in a class by itself, the former Poellnitzia rublflora has been classified as Astroloba. It is a distinct, imposing and very unusual succulent that produces equally impressive red flowers.

Euphorbia
Euphorbiaceae genus

Place of Origin: Africa, Madagascar, etc.
Growth Difficulty: 2/3
Type: Summer, Spring-Fall, Winter
Watering: Unlike other succulents, they are weak to dry environments, so give them plenty of water during their growth periods. Avoid letting them get too dry during their dormancy by watering them occasionally.

Characteristics Euphorbia is a large genus of plants that grows in many regions of the world, from tropical to temperate. They are commonly known to have about 500 varieties in cultivation. The stems and branches of these plants have evolved to become succulent in response to their various harsh environments.

Tips for Cultivation Details vary depending on the original habitat of each variety, but in general they should be placed in a sunny and well-ventilated environment. For cold-sensitive species, move them indoors during winter. They are generally more susceptible to drought than other succulents, so be careful not to let them dry out completely during the dormant season.

Euphorbia aeruginosa

It grows as a group of thin, celadon-colored trunks with rows of glossy, copper-colored spikes that line up in order.

Summer **13 cm**

Euphorbia alluaudii ssp. onconclada

It's unique for its slender, elongated stems and very small leaves. Although it grows flowers, many Euphorbia species are dioecious (have separate sexes), and their flowers need to be matched in order to pollinate and produce fruit.

Summer **10 cm**

Euphorbia alluaudii ssp. onconclada f. cristata

Its stem growth point is affected and causes this crested variant to grow in an unusual way.

Summer **9 cm**

Euphorbia bupleurifolia

The bumps on the trunk, which make it look like pineapple skin, are actually the marks left by leaves that fell in winter. It is sensitive to high humidity, so keep it in a well-ventilated place in the rainy season and in summer.

Spring-Fall **11 cm**

Euphorbia clandestina

Summer | **10 cm**

A knobby columnar that produces small red flowers. As it grows, the upper part becomes thicker and tufty.

Euphorbia cooperi

Summer | **10 cm**

One of the euphorbia varieties that have lost their leaves and have only a trunk. Its growth is fast. It produces toxic sap so be careful when handling it.

Euphorbia decaryi

Summer | **11 cm**

It grows branches and tuberous roots under its leaves. Although its seedlings are available for purchase, it's an endangered species.

Euphorbia enopla f. monstrosa

Summer | **9 cm**

It has spikes all over its body. As it grows, the upper part becomes thicker and the spines grow brighter.

Euphorbia flanaganii

Summer | **13 cm**

Commonly called Medusa Plant, this is one of several varieties that grow into many separate branches. A few times a year, it grows small yellow flowers on the tips of its branches.

Euphorbia 'Gabizan'

Summer | **10 cm**

The uneven part of the leaves comes from its hybrid parent, Euphorbia bupleurifolia. It is sensitive to high summer temperatures, humidity, and direct sunlight.

Euphorbia globosa

Summer | **10 cm**

Produces round branches that look like puffy balls. It grows into this unique pile-of-balls shape.

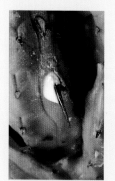

Euphorbia enopla f. monstrosa

NOTE

Euphorbia's white sap

Most Euphorbias produce a highly toxic sap. The white sap that seeps out when the roots, stems or leaves are damaged contains substances that irritate the skin and eyes. So please be careful when handling them.

* Avoid direct contact with skin and eyes.
* If you get sap on your skin, wash it off immediately with soap and water.
* If you are going to cut a tree, wipe off the sap from the trunk or roots, or rinse it off with water, and then dry the cut end thoroughly.
* Make sure you are in a well-ventilated area when handling Euphorbias

Euphorbia golisana

Long red spines cover the entire plant. It grows in clusters to form what looks like a miniature forest of spines.

Summer **8 cm**

Euphorbia guillauminiana

Summer **14 cm**

It loses its foliage in winter. After spring, leaves begin to reappear and it produces flowers. It does not tolerate high humidity from the rainy season to summer and is also susceptible to the cold in winter.

Euphorbia horrida

Summer **8 cm**

The spikes are leftover flower stalks after its flower stems fall off. It doesn't handle direct sunlight well, so it should be grown in half-shade.

Euphorbia inconstantia

Summer **12 cm**

The spherical shape of Euphorbia trunks can hold a lot of water, so water only when the soil is completely dry.

Euphorbia inermis

Summer **12 cm**

Like the Medusa Plant, it produces flowers on the tips of its branches. With all of these "fingerly" Euphorbia, water only when the soil is completely dry. Too much water leads to stretching, and the branches grow thin.

Euphorbia lactea f. cristata

Summer **11 cm**

A crested variant of Euphorbia lactea with a band of growth points. It has many variations such as white ones, red ones and even speckled ones.

Euphorbia lactea f. cristata

Summer **11 cm**

A variant with cream-colored speckles.

Euphorbia lactea *'White Ghost'*

A bleached variety of Euphorbia lactea. New shoots start out pink and gradually turn white. It's pretty hardy and easy to grow.

Summer **9 cm**

Euphorbia mammillaris f. variegata

Spring-Fall | **8 cm**

A speckled variety of Euphorbia mammillaris. The lack of pigmentation makes it weak to strong sunlight, so be careful in midsummer.

Euphorbia milii

Summer | **12 cm**

This evergreen shrub is covered in thorns and can flower for extremely long periods. New variants are constantly being discovered, and each one has its own characteristics.

Euphorbia: Rich in individuality

NOTE

The genus Euphorbia is a large group of plants distributed in various parts of the world. It is said to have approximately 2,000 varieties in total. Among those, only 500 -1,000 species are actually categorized as succulents. Because they have evolved into forms and shapes suited to surviving each of their native habitats, they are so unique and varied that it is hard to believe that they all belong to the same genus.

Euphorbia mauritanica

Summer | **11 cm**

Euphorbia mauritanica is one of the green-branched Euphorbia species, with very few leaves and a multitude thin of branches.

Euphorbia milii cv. Horticultural variant

Summer | **12 cm**

Milii lovers the world over have produced many cultivated variants and hybrids. Their flowers can vary from pinks to reds, and creamy shades to yellow.

Euphorbia obesa

Summer | **10 cm**

Round and almost pleated in shape, with a checkered pattern. The sculpted look and distinct pattern make it hard to believe that this is a work of nature.

Euphorbia meloformis ssp. valida

Summer | **8 cm**

This ribbed, round dwarf has characteristic stripes. It also blow its seedlings very far afield. After flowering, the withered floret remains and withers.

Euphorbia milii hyb. Hybrid variant

Summer | **9 cm**

The spines are covering the plant all over and it grows lovely flowers. These varieties tend to have gummy sap, so be sure to tend to your skin and your tools after trimming.

Euphorbia obesa ssp. symmetrica

Summer | **10 cm**

Slightly flatter than Euphorbia obesa. Its spherical body is filled with water inside. Be careful to not overwater them.

Euphorbia obesa ssp. symmetrica

Summer | **10 cm**

The obesa family is characterized by the ability to grow offspring through the ridges around the parent sphere.

Euphorbia polygona

Summer | **8 cm**

While very similar in appearance, Euphorbia polygona differs from Euphorbia horrida in the black-purple color of its flowers and its higher ridge count.

Euphorbia pseudoglobosa

Summer | **7 cm**

The knobby globular leaves grow densely. They are weak to high humidity. Use a fan or similar during hot and humid periods to keep moisture from accumulating.

Euphorbia 'Sotetsukirin'

Summer | **10 cm**

The plant in the photo is 5–6 years old. It grows slowly and can resemble a tree or, depending on the growth pattern of the stem, a pineapple.

Euphorbia submamillaris

Summer | **8 cm**

This densely-branched dwarf shrub is one of the smaller euphorbia varieties It produces a lot of offspring that grow in clusters from the base of the plant.

Euphorbia venenifica ssp. poissonii

Summer | **12 cm**

A variant of Euphorbia venenifica, the parent of many hybrids. The tips of the leaves have slightly wavy serrations.

Cactus spines and Euphorbia spines

Many members of the Euphorbia genus have spines that look like those of the cactus family. The key to distinguishing them is that the spines of the cactus family have an organ called a stigma. The stigma is the white, fluff-like area at the base of the spine, which was originally a deformed short branch. Even cacti without spines have stigmas. Euphorbia spines do not have stigmas.

There are also differences in the way their spines are formed. Cacti spines are thought to be mainly transformed "stipules." It is thought that they evolved into spines in order to minimize the transpiration of water from the leaves and to protect the plants from predators.

NOTE

couperii (Euphorbia)   **hannya (Cactaceae)**

The Euphorbia genus is composed of a variety of species, that have also evolved in different ways, including varieties with cactus-like altered stipules and others with hardened flower stems that remain after the flowers have finished blooming.

Monadenium
Euphorbiaceae genus

Place of Origin: Africa, etc.
Growth Difficulty: 2/3
Type: Summer, Spring-Fall
Watering: Unlike other succulents, they are weak to dry environments, so give them plenty of water during their growth periods. Water them occasionally during dormancy so that they won't dry out.

Characteristics A genus very close to Euphorbia. There are varieties with fleshy and warty stems, others have completely lost leaves, and some grow their tuberous roots to very large sizes.

Tips for Cultivation Like Euphorbia, many varieties have weak rooting and are susceptible to drought. Water them several times a month, even during their dormancy in winter; if they remain without water for too long the roots will weaken. Move them indoors in a bright environment during winter.

Monadenium ellenbeckii

`Summer` `10 cm`

Its branches grows into asparagus-like stems. Can be bred by simply planting cut branches.

Monadenium guentheri

`Summer` `8 cm`

It has a bumpy green trunk that grows upward to 16–20"/40–50cm in height. White flowers grow on its tips.

Monadenium schubei 'Tanzania Red'

`Spring-Fall` `10 cm`

Two-toned white and red flowers bloom from September to December. The reddish-purple trunk is also beautiful.

Monadenium ritchiei

`Summer` `10 cm`

The leaves emerge from the bumpy, whipped-like trunk in early summer, but fall off quickly, only to be followed by the blooming of small pink flowers. It is sensitive to direct sunlight in midsummer, and the leaves may get burned, so use a shade net or similar.

Monadenium sp.

`Spring-Fall` `11 cm`

Species whose Japanese name most closely romanizes as "decaldeae." Pale cream-green with white speckles and pink leaves. It produces offspring frequently.

Pedilanthus
Euphorbiaceae genu

Place of Origin: Africa
Growth Difficulty: 2/3
Type: Summer **Watering:** Unlike other succulents, they are weak to dry environments, so give them plenty of water during their growth periods. Water them occasionally during dormancy so that they won't dry out.

Characteristics & Tips for Cultivation
Basically, you want to follow the same rules as Euphorbia. Grow in full sun throughout the year. Give plenty of water when the soil dries out during the growing season from May to September. Water occasionally during the dormant season too. When the temperatures start to increase, also gradually increase the amount of watering.

Summer **8 cm**

The entire plant is covered with white powder and the leaves are also covered with white spots, giving this plant an indescribable beauty. Its Japanese name is "Oogiryuu," which means "Great Silver Dragon" and, indeed, the plant has both power and grace.

Pedilanthus smallii nana '*Milk Harmony*'

Jatropha
Euphorbiaceae genus

Place of Origin: Central Asia, Eastern Indian Archipelago, etc.
Growth Difficulty: 2/3
Type: Summer **Watering:** Give plenty of water when the soil is completely dry. No watering during winter.

Characteristics & Tips for Cultivation
They are sensitive to cold, so when the minimum temperature falls below 59°F/15°C, move them indoors to a bright spot. When the leaves begin to fall, reduce watering little by little, and once all the leaves have fallen, stop watering altogether. In early spring, when the leaves start to emerge, gradually begin watering and continue to water all the way through summer.

Summer **15 cm**

It's characterized by round and plentiful tuberous roots and leaves with deep cuts. It grows coral pink flowers in summer.

Jatropha berlandieri

Lithops

Aizoaceae genus

Place of Origin: Southern Africa
Growth Difficulty: 1/3
Type: Winter
Watering: Between fall and spring, water generously when the soil dries up. After that gradually reduce watering to almost none during they dormancy in summer.

Characteristics The two leaves combined with a single stem create a mysterious form. It is said that these plants have evolved to mimic stones to avoid being eaten by animals. They are also nicknamed "living gems" because of their beautiful patterns and colors.

Tips for Cultivation The key to good growth is to expose them to full sun from fall to spring and keep them in a well-ventilated location. During spring, when the old leaves break off and begin to molt, water sparingly to prevent double molting, which can also cause newer growth to wither.

Lithops aucampiae

| Winter | 6 cm |

It combines a reddish-brown window color with brown reticulation. They are hardy and easy to grow even for beginners.

Lithops aucampiae *'Jackson's Jade'*

| Winter | 7 cm |

A variant of the aucampiae with yellow skin and yellow flowers.

Lithops bromfieldii

| Winter | 6 cm |

This variant has a very austere color, but there are many varieties of Phellodendron bromfieldii, including reddish purple and yellow variants.

Lithops bromfieldii var. glaudinae

This is another variety with a subdued coloring. It grows yellow flowers in fall.

| Winter |
| 6 cm |

Lithops fulviceps *'Aurea'*

A mutated variant of Lithops fulviceps. It has a pale yellow-green window color with dark green dots. The name means "golden," but it grows white flowers in fall.

| Winter |
| 6 cm |

Lithops hallii

It's a variety with many fans thanks to its beautiful red-orange speckles. It is believed to be a selected variety of Lithops hallii, but there are many unknown details about this variety. It grows white flowers in fall.

Winter **6 cm**

Lithops helmutii

Winter **6 cm**

A variety with leaves that split in two. It is characterized by its translucent blue-gray leaf color.

Lithops hookeri

Winter **6 cm**

It has a characteristic brain-like reticulate pattern. There are many varieties and sub-species with a variety of colors and patterns.

Lithops hookeri var. subfenestrata 'Brunneoviolacea'

Winter **6 cm**

A purple-brown variant of hookeri. The pattern on the window part is slightly colored by the leaf's base color.

Lithops julii

Winter **6 cm**

There are many varieties of Lithops julii, with a wide variety of colors and patterns. It grows white flowers.

Lithops julii 'Reticulate'

Winter **6 cm**

It has a gray window color with a clear reddish-brown pattern.

Lithops julii ssp. fulleri 'Kosogyoku'

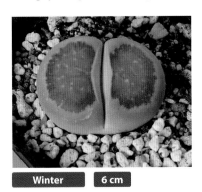

Winter **6 cm**

The pattern is not easily visible and is matte red in color. It grows large white flowers in winter.

Lithops julii ssp. fulleri var. 'Fuller-green'

Winter **6 cm**

A variant of 'Fukuroigatama' that has turned green. White flowers emerge from the emerald green plants.

Lithops karasmontana *'Syusingyoku'*

An improved variant of karasmontana, with a striking bright red pattern. It grows white flowers.

Winter
6 cm

Lithops karasmontana *'Topred'*

It is characterized by its distinct red reticulate pattern.

Winter
6 cm

Lithops lesliei ssp. lesliei var. *'Albinica'*

A variant of the standard Lithops 'Purple lesliei'. It's characterized by the bright yellow color pattern on the window.

Winter
6 cm

Lithops lesliei *'Grey'*

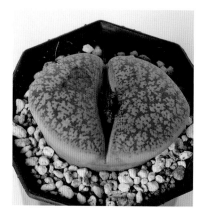

It has a grayish green pattern. The colors and patterns of Lithops can vary considerably from plant to plant.

Winter
6 cm

Lithops lesliei var. rubrobrunnea

It has a reddish-bronze window with deep purple pattern.

Winter
6 cm

Lithops localis *'Peersii'*

The top of the plant is rounded and swollen, with 6 to 8 separate heads. It has a pale peach-gray window with a dotted pattern.

Winter
6 cm

Lithops marmorata

Winter **6 cm**

The plump, rounded shape is lovely. It grows white flowers from fall to winter (see the hybrid plants a lower right.)

Lithops naureeniae

Winter **6 cm**

The contrast between the light maroon and grayish green is elegant. It grows yellow flowers in fall.

Lithops pseudotruncatella

Winter **7 cm**

Mimics quartzite's colors. It has a grayish-brown window with small cracks and a pattern of branches and dots.

Lithops schwanteesii

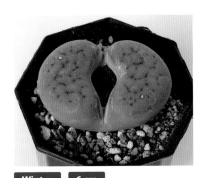

Winter **6 cm**

A whitish tinted variety. There are many variants and subspecies of schwanteesii with different colors, but they are all generally pale.

Lithops hybrids

Winter **9 cm**

These are "hybrids" whose hybrid parents are unknown or whose names are unknown because their tags have been lost. The shape of the leaves and the tint/pattern of the window at the top are slightly different for each individual plant. Also, while their flowers have the same color, the shape of their corollas is slightly different. It can be fun to try to guess who the hybrid parents are if you happen to get one.

NOTE

New shoots are sprouting from the center of stretched-out Lithops

Lithops Stretching: Wait for the next molt

In order to grow Lithops in a nice shape, so that they can stand low like a pedestal, it is important to expose them to plenty of sunlight during the growing season from fall to spring. If they lack sunlight or ventilation during this period, the plant will weaken and grow upward.

If this happens, you shouldn't trim the plant or repot it as in other succulents. Instead, patiently wait for the next "molt" and until then, keep the plants in a well-ventilated location in half-shade during the dormant season in summer. From fall to spring, keep the plants in full sun and patiently wait for the next molt, if you're patient, new and strong shoots will grow in the following year.

Conophytum
Aizoaceae genus

Place of Origin: Southern Africa
Growth Difficulty: 2/3
Type: Winter
Watering: From fall to spring, give plenty of water when the soil dries out. After spring, gradually reduce watering, stopping almost entirely in midsummer during their dormant period.

Characteristics As the photos indicate, these puffy, dumpling-shaped plants are very small. Essentially, they consist of a pair of leaves that fuse together, retaining a slit between them. They also grow brightly colored flowers which reach upward as they pop open, making them a very popular genus, with many garden varieties being grown.

Tips for Cultivation Like Lithops, this genus grows by molting. The plants are small and will die if they lack water during the dormant summer months, so give them a little water about twice a month. When normal watering is resumed in fall, new shoots emerge from among the old leaves. Keep indoors in a very bright environment during winter.

Conophytum ectypum ssp. brownii

A small, clustered sub-variant of Ectypum. It has reddish-purple stripes and grows pale pink flowers.

Winter
6 cm

Conophytum ficiforme

Its leaves are the color of young grass and are strewn with reddish-purple dots. It grows flowers in clusters that have a beautiful gradation of reddish-purple and white.

Winter
7 cm

Conophytum flavum

It's saddle-shaped, often growing in clusters. It has muscat green leaves with small translucent dots at the top.

Winter
8 cm

Conophytum flavum ssp. novicium

It's a night-blooming variant of Conophytum flavum. It has a simpler appearance to that of day-blooming flowers, but it produces a fragrance that attracts insects.

Winter
7 cm

Conophytum gratum

Winter **6 cm**

Looks like a flattened pebble. It has semi-transparent dots and grows bright pink flowers.

Conophytum herreaonthus

Winter **7 cm**

It has large leaves that split to the left and right and grow alternately. Formerly was classified in its own Herreanthus.

Conophytum luisae

Winter **6 cm**

Shallow bean-like shapes with reddish-purple drops on the top. It grows yellow flowers in fall.

Conophytum minimum 'Notatum'

Winter **7 cm**

The color of its dots is similar to the reddish purple at the base of the plant, with a bruise-like pattern at the top.

Conophytum minimum 'Wittebergense'

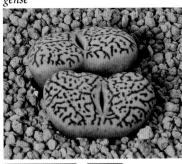

Winter **7 cm**

Conophytum minimum has many variants and subspecies of different colors and patterns. 'Wittebergense' is characterized by its beautiful arabesque pattern in deep purple.

Conophytum obcordellum 'Mundum'

Winter **7 cm**

A beautiful contrast of purple and yellowish green. It's a horticultural variant of obcordellum.

Conophytum obcordellum 'N. Vredendal'

Winter **10 cm**

The dead flowers on the leaves may leave marks on the plant, so it is best to remove the flower petals as soon as possible.

Conophytum occultum

Winter **6 cm**

A cute variety with small heart-shaped leaves growing in clusters.

Conophytum pearsonii

Winter **6 cm**

It grows pink flowers so large that they obscure the leaves in the fall. The leaves have almost no pattern.

Conophytum pellucidum '3km Concordia'

Winter **7 cm**

A variant of the pellucidum family, which has a wide variety of variants and subspecies in terms of color, pattern, and shape.

Conophytum pellucidum var. neohallii

Winter **7 cm**

The most basic variant of Neohallii. It's green with a beige pattern. It has many variants with different colors.

Conophytum pubescens 'W Platbakkies'

Winter **7 cm**

A horticultural variety of Conophytum pubescens which lacks the fine hairs of the original species. It has a large transparent window in the middle of the leaves.

Conophytum 'Shukuten'

Winter **10 cm**

It's made of many pairs of heart-shaped leaves growing in clusters facing each other. It grows orange flowers.

Conophytum 'Shukuten'

Winter **10 cm**

A shukuten variant. Its flowers have a beautiful gradation of white to pink.

Conophytum 'Suitekidama'

Winter **10 cm**

A cute variety that grows in clusters of small leaf pairs. They require care to prevent steaming. They grow wisteria-colored flowers in fall.

Conophytum 'Sunline'

Winter **13 cm**

It has a red line on the tips of the leaves. It grows small yellow flowers.

Conophytum truncatum 'Subglobosum'

Winter **8 cm**

It looks very similar to other truncatum variants, bit translucent dot pattern on the leaves stands out.

Conophytum uviforme

Winter **8 cm**

It grows puffy heart-shapes and has a stitch-like pattern. It grows night-blooming white flowers with a nice fragrance.

Conophytum uviforme 'Hillii'

Winter **8 cm**

It has dot patterns throughout and a stitched pattern on the upper part.

Conophytum bilobun

Winter **10 cm**

Similar in appearance to Conophytum velutinum, the flowers that grow on this species might be orange, yellow or purple.

Conophytum 'Zushiou'

Winter **8 cm**

The patterns on the upper part are uneven which makes them look bumpy. It grows white night-blooming flowers.

PETIT

Obtaining Succulents: Conophytum and Lithops skin molting/shedding

Conophytum's yearly cycle

Early summer (late May - early June) The leaves gradually wrinkle and the skin turns brown.

Summer (July-August) The plant appears to be dead, but it is really just laying dormant with a brown skin.

Early fall (early September)

During the growing season, new shoots emerge, breaking through the brown withered skin.

1. Increase watering little by little.
2. Then, remove the shed skin.

1 The old skin has withered.

2 Pinch off the old skin with tweezers, being careful not to damage the new leaves.

3 Remove the dead flower buds as well.

4 You can pull them out smoothly upward.

5 The Conophytum now looks nice and clean.

Lithops' yearly cycle

Early spring (around February) Leaves start to wrinkle, it's the first sign of molting.

Spring (mid-April) The old leaves split in two, revealing new leaves inside.

Summer (June-July)

1. Old leaves wither and new leaves emerge from within.
2. Remove the shed skin.

1 Lithops's old leaves do not wither as much as conophytum's, but they stand in the way of new leaves nonetheless.

2 Pinch off the old skin with tweezers, being careful not to damage the new leaves.

3 You can remove old skin by gently pulling upward.

Aloinopsis
Aizoaceae genus

Place of Origin: Southern Africa, etc. **Growth Difficulty:** 1/3
Type: Winter **Watering:** In summer, when the plant is dormant, water it only a few times a month, just enough to wet the soil around it. In other seasons, water generously when the soil is dry.

Characteristics & Tips for Cultivation
Native to south Africa and other regions with close to no rain. The fleshy leaves are often covered with small indentations to better absorb nutrients. Keep in a sunny, well-ventilated location. They are sensitive to humidity, so they should be kept in a well-ventilated areas with some shelter against the rain. In winter, move them indoors if the temperature drops below 32F°/0°C to avoid frost.

Aloinopsis malherbei

It has large, gracefully spreading leaves. The white protuberances on the tips look feathery. It grows large cream-colored flowers.

Winter

8 cm

Aloinopsis orpeni

The thick, yet shimmering shape of the leaves is characteristic of this variety. Leaves have small white bumps all over them.

Winter

8 cm

Antegibbaeum
Aizoaceae genus

Place of Origin: Southern Africa **Growth Difficulty:** 2/3
Type: Winter **Watering:** In summer, when the plant is dormant, water it only a few times a month, just enough to wet the soil around it. In other seasons, water generously when the soil is dry.

Characteristics & Tips for Cultivation
Native to the dry, sandy gravel soils of South Africa. They do not tolerate high temperatures and humidity, so protect them during the rainy season and through midsummer. During these periods, grow them in half-shade or use shade nets. They are resistant to cold and can be grown outdoors year round in some regions.

Antegibbaeum fissoide

The leaves are arranged and spread in pairs. The outside of the leaves has wrinkles that look like the skin of an elephant.

Winter

7 cm

Ihlenfeldtia
Aizoaceae genus

Place of Origin: Southern Africa **Growth Difficulty:** 2/3
Type: Winter **Watering:** In summer, when the plant is dormant, water it only a few times a month, just enough to wet the soil around it. In other seasons, water generously when the soil is dry.

Characteristics & Tips for Cultivation
A recent genus separated from Cheiridopsis. It does not tolerate high temperatures and humidity, so be careful from the beginning of the rainy season to midsummer. During this period, mostly reduce watering, and keep them in half-shade or protect with shade nets. Quite resistant to cold.

Ihlenfeldtia vanzylii

The leaves have elephant skin-like wrinkles and leaves that look like mussels. It grows bright yellow flowers.

Winter

8 cm

Phyllobolus

Aizoaceae genus

Place of Origin: Southern Africa
Growth Difficulty: 1/3
Type: Winter **Watering:** In summer, when the plant is dormant, water it only a few times a month, just enough to wet the soil around it. In other seasons, water generously when the soil is dry.

Characteristics & Tips for Cultivation

A genus native to high plains and rocky areas in South Africa. The fleshy leaf surface is covered with tiny protuberances that store minerals and salts. Take extra care in the period between the rainy season and midsummer. During this period, water should be cut off and the plant should be kept in semi-shade or protected with a shade nets. Although it can tolerate cold, water sparingly in winter and move indoors when temperatures fall below 32F°/0°C.

Phyllobolus resurgens

A caudex with a thick trunk. The branches grow in all directions from the trunk. Leaves have small, flattened surfaces.

`Winter` `8 cm`

Phyllobolus tenuiflorus

A caudex with a thick trunk. The branches and flower stems tend to grow horizontally. It has velvety hairs on the flower stems. Its leaves fall during the dormant season.

`Winter` `7 cm`

Pleiospilos

Aizoaceae genus

Place of Origin: Southern Africa
Growth Difficulty: 1/3 **Type:** Winter **Watering:** In summer, when the plant is dormant, water it only a few times a month, just enough to wet the soil around it. In other seasons, water generously when the soil is dry.

Characteristics & Tips for Cultivation

This is a species with stony leaves that are full of water, a typical trait of the Aizoaceae family. Being winter types, they grow in the colder months before the start of spring. They are susceptible to high temperatures and humidity, so be careful during the rainy season and over midsummer. Keep in full sunlight during their growing season in the colder months. From the onset of the rainy season to midsummer, reduce watering and move to half-shade. It is prone to having pests, so it should be repotted regularly.

Pleiospilos nelii

Has two hemispherical, thick-walled leaves with small green spots on their surface. It grows large orange flowers.

`Winter` `8 cm`

Pleiospilos nelii *'Royal Flush'*

A garden variety of Pleiospilos nelii with purple leaves. It grows dark pink flowers. It grows hardly any offspring, so it is has to be bred by seeds.

`Winter` `8 cm`

Argyroderma
Aizoaceae genus

Place of Origin: Southern Africa **Growth Difficulty:** 1/3
Type: Winter **Watering:** In summer, when the plant is dormant, water it only a few times a month, just enough to wet the soil around it. In other seasons, water generously when the soil is dry.

Characteristics & Tips for Cultivation
The name of the genus means "silvery-white leaves" in Latin. It does not tolerate high temperatures and humidity in summer, so make sure to take appropriate care. During their growing season, they might split if exposed to high humidity, so they should be kept in a well-ventilated place. When the temperatures fall below 32°F/ 0°C, move them indoors to a bright spot.

Argyroderma delaetii

Its flower color varies from red, pink, yellow, and white, depending on the individual plant. The flowers are large and similar to gerberas.

Winter **8 cm**

Oscularia deltoides

It grows as a shrub with small, serrated leaves. The leaves turn red during fall and winter when exposed to full sun. It grows pink flowers.

Winter **11 cm**

Oscularia
Aizoaceae genus

Place of Origin: Southern Africa **Growth Difficulty:** 3/3
Type: Winter **Watering:** In summer, when the plant is dormant, water it only a few times a month, just enough to wet the soil around it. In other seasons, water generously when the soil is dry.

Characteristics & Tips for Cultivation
This is a small genus with only a few species native to the Cape Peninsula of South Africa. The stems tend to branch out and become shrub-like as they gradually become woody. They are relatively cold-tolerant, hardy, and easy to grow among the Aizoaceae, which are usually susceptible to extreme winters despite being generally resistant to cold.

Glottiphyllum
Aizoaceae genus

Place of Origin: Southern Africa **Growth Difficulty:** 3/3
Type: Winter **Watering:** In summer, when the plant is dormant, water it only a few times a month, just enough to wet the soil around it. In other seasons, water generously when the soil is dry.

Characteristics & Tips for Cultivation
About 60 species have been identified in South Africa. It has three-lobed leaves growing into tongue shapes. It is relatively resistant to both hot and cold temperatures, and can be grown outdoors in a mild winter. They like good light, good soil drainage, and good ventilation.

Glottiphyllum nelii

The wide leaves form a fan-like shape. The contrast between the yellow flowers and muscat green leaves is beautiful in the fall.

Winter **10 cm**

Stomatium
Aizoaceae genus

Place of Origin: Southern Africa **Growth Difficulty:** 1/3
Type: Winter **Watering:** In summer, when the plant is dormant, water it only a few times a month, just enough to wet the soil around it. In other seasons, water generously when the soil is dry.

Characteristics & Tips for Cultivation
In general they are sturdy and easy to grow but are susceptible to high heat and humidity, so grow in a well-ventilated, half-shade during summer. It grows best when it stays at temperatures between 41 and 68°F (5 and 20°C). When temperatures drop below 41°F/5°C, move indoors to a bright spot.

Stomatium duthieae

The leaves are covered with small spikes, with the tips tightly serrated. The leaves also are cross-shaped and neatly paired.

Winter 10 cm

Titanopsis schwantesii *'Primosii'*

It has pentagonal or hexagonal white protuberances on the tips of its leaves. These are used to store minerals and salts. It grows yellow flowers in spring and early summer.

Winter 10 cm

Titanopsis
Aizoaceae genus

Place of Origin: Southern Africa **Growth Difficulty:** 2/3
Type: Winter **Watering:** In summer, when the plant is dormant, water it only a few times a month, just enough to wet the soil around it. In other seasons, water generously when the soil is dry.

Characteristics & Tips for Cultivation
Native to dry and arid regions in South Africa, where rainfall is scarce. After watering, it is important to allow the soil to dry out thoroughly. The tips of its leaves are covered with crushed leaves that store minerals and salt in order to survive harsh environments.

Dinteranthus
Aizoaceae genus

Place of Origin: Southern Africa **Growth Difficulty:** 3/3
Type: Winter **Watering:** In summer, when the plant is dormant, water it only a few times a month, just enough to wet the soil around it. In other seasons, water generously when the soil is dry.

Characteristics & Tips for Cultivation
Besides appearances, it shares some characteristics of Lithops, including molting. Keep in a well-lit, well-ventilated location away from rain and frost throughout the year. In hot and humid summers, move to half-shade or use shade nets to cover the plants. In summer, use a fan to cut back on humidity.

Dinteranthus vanzylii

The plant in the photo is still young so has no pattern on it yet, but when it grows, it will have a braided pattern similar to a Lithops.

Winter 7 cm

Trichodiadema
Aizoaceae genus

Place of Origin: Southern Africa **Growth Difficulty:** 3/3
Type: Winter **Watering:** In summer, when the plant is dormant, water it only a few times a month, just enough to wet the soil around it. In other seasons, water generously when the soil is dry.

Characteristics & Tips for Cultivation
About fifty species of Trichodiadema are distributed over a wide area in South Africa. It is characterized by small, narrow leaves with thin spines at the tips. It is one of the caudex varieties whose rhizomes (the roots just barely under the surface of the soil) enlarge as it grows. It is relatively resistant to cold and, well cared-for, can grow for many years to come.

Trichodiadema sp. White fl.

It is also called a natural bonsai. As it grows, the trunk, branches, and roots become thicker, producing an interesting branching pattern.

Winter | **7 cm**

Nananthus sp.

Small spots can be seen all over the leaves. It may not look strong now, but in a few years it will grow into a great caudex.

Winter | **7 cm**

Nananthus
Aizoaceae genus

Place of Origin: Southern Africa **Growth Difficulty:** 1/3
Type: Winter **Watering:** In summer, when the plant is dormant, water it only a few times a month, just enough to wet the soil around it. In other seasons, water generously when the soil is dry.

Characteristics & Tips for Cultivation
Their leaves are fleshy and triangular when looked at in cross-section. They grow very slowly but as they grow, the rhizome part enlarges and becomes very caudex-like. They are rare species, with only about ten varieties growing in the wild in central South Africa.

Echinus
Aizoaceae genus

Place of Origin: Southern Africa **Growth Difficulty:** 1/3
Type: Winter **Watering:** In summer, when the plant is dormant, water it only a few times a month, just enough to wet the soil around it. In other seasons, water generously when the soil is dry.

Characteristics & Tips for Cultivation
This is a rare family, with only five varieties known from the southern African regions. They are susceptible to high summer temperatures and humidity, so in summer, keep them in a well-ventilated, half-shaded location and water them as little as possible. In winter, it should be placed in a location that can maintain a temperature of 32°F/ 0°C or higher. Some consider them to be classifiable members of the genus Braunsia.

Echinus maximiliani

Echinus maximiliani is a popular variety because of the charming appearance of its leaves and flowers, and for its graceful "trail." It is rather difficult to grow and requires good care. It likes to be watered, so give water generously as soon as the soil dries out.

Winter | **12 cm**

Frithia
Aizoaceae genus

Place of Origin: Southern Africa **Growth Difficulty:** 1/3
Type: Summer **Watering:** Water generously when the soil is dry. Moderate watering during the dormancy in winter.

Characteristics & Tips for Cultivation
Summer-type plants are rare in the Aizoaceae family. Be careful to control temperatures in their environment. In winter, when temperatures fall below 41°F/5°C, move the plant indoors in full sun and water only in moderation. Otherwise, keep in a sunny, well-ventilated location outdoors except in midsummer.

Frithia pulchra

The entire surface of the rod-shaped leaves is covered in white spots, including the windows on the upper sections. Expose to plenty of sunlight through all seasons except midsummer.

Summer **10 cm**

Bergeranthus
Aizoaceae genus

Place of Origin: Southern Africa **Growth Difficulty:** 2/3
Type: Winter **Watering:** In summer, when the plant is dormant, water it only a few times a month, just enough to wet the soil around it. In other seasons, water generously when the soil is dry.

Characteristics & Tips for Cultivation
A strong and hardy variety that naturally grows in the arid regions of South Africa. Its leaves are full of water well. It is relatively resistant to cold and can survive mild winters outdoors

Bergeranthus multiceps f. variegata

The new shoots are lime green in color but turn to a more somber shade once they are fully grown. The long, slender, and spiny leaves grow in clusters.

Winter **8 cm**

Ruschia
Aizoaceae genus

Place of Origin: Southern Africa **Growth Difficulty:** 2/3
Type: Spring-Fall **Watering:** In summer, when the plant is dormant, water it only once a month. In other seasons, water generously when the soil is dry.

Characteristics & Tips for Cultivation
A small species native to South Africa. It has a dormant period in winter and a semi-dormant period in summer. It is relatively resistant to the cold and can be grown outdoors where winters are mild. The key is to keep it in a well-ventilated place where it will not be exposed to rain.

Ruschia indurata

The small but fleshy leaves grow in crossed pairs, giving the impression of being neatly arranged. It can be bred by separating the offspring or grown from seedlings.

Spring-Fall
7 cm

Agave

Asparagaceae genus

Place of Origin: Central-South America, mainly Mexico
Growth Difficulty: 3/3
Type: Summer
Watering: From spring to fall water generously when the soil is dry. In winter reduce the frequency to about once a month, and give less water.

Characteristics Each variety has its own unique appearance, with some having sharp spikes at the tips of their leaves, others having slender, tidy leaves, and others having beautiful, speckled patterns. Different varieties have been used to treat wounds, prevent infection, make soap, sweeten tea and more.

Tips for Cultivation Its natural habitat is arid, so try to avoid exposing them to rain during the rainy season and use fans or similar methods to deal with midsummer humidity. Some types are quite resistant to cold and can be planted outdoors, while others are less tolerant to cold (keep indoors in full sun when temperatures drop below 41°F/5°C).

Agave americana

`Summer` `10 cm`

It can grow to be over 10'/3m in height in its native habitat. It is highly resistant to cold weather. Prefers full sun but can tolerate mild shade.

Agave *'Burnt Burgundy'*

`Summer` `15 cm`

The burgundy-red edge decorating the slender leaves looks stylish and fashionable. Like all agaves it likes good drainage, and will grow well in gravely soil.

Agave bovicornuta

`Summer` `10 cm`

The reddish-brown spines give it a wild look. The wide leaves with large curves give it an appealing shape. Over time the rosette can grow to just over 39"/1m tall, and 59"/1.5m in diameter.

Agave *'Celsii Nova'*

`Summer` `10 cm`

The reddish-brown spikes on the edges of its leaves and the bluish foliage give it an elegant look. It grows plenty of offspring.

NOTE

Water marks and growth marks in Agave

Agaves and other succulents sometimes have white stains or smudges on their leaves. These are "water marks," traces left by water that was accumulated on the leaves during watering and has evaporated (Avoid watering the leaves as much as possible).

However, there is another pattern of smudges on agave that differs from water marks. I'm referring to the small arched lines that can be seen in the center of the leaves (see the photo on the right). These are marks left by the plant's own growth. The spike marks are caused by the scrubbing between leaves and spikes that happened during the plant's growth. Those marks cannot be removed. It is tempting to scrub them clean, but never try to scrub them off, as this will damage the leaves.

Agave 'Blue Emperor'

`Summer` `13 cm`

The black spines surrounding the leaves and the deep green foliage give it a dark, subdued look.

Agave dasylirioides

`Summer` `12 cm`

A beautiful variety that has almost no spines and pretty slender leaves.

Agave difformis

`Summer` `15 cm`

The stripes on the outside of the leaves look as if they have been hand-drawn with a pen. There are also variants with black spines.

Agave filifera ssp. multifilifera

`Summer` `10 cm`

The filifera group is characterized by the white thread-like filaments that form around the leaves.

Agave geminiflora

`Summer` `14 cm`

Thelong, narrow leaves are attached by filaments. The supple spreading leaves and filaments create a dynamic atmosphere.

Agave ghiesbreghtii

`Summer` `10 cm`

It has thick, stiff leaves. The tips of the leaves and the spines on the edges are sharp.

Agave gigantensis 'Rancho Soledad'

`Summer` `10 cm`

It has gray-green leaves with brown spines on the edges. The rosette can grow to about 3'/1m in both diameter and grass height

Agave isthmensis

Despite being less than 12"/30 cm in diameter, it has a very imposing form. It is very similar to Potatorum and can sometimes confused with it. Agave isthmensis has shorter leaves, wavy tips on the spikes surrounding the leaves, deeper serrations, and also has a more rugged overall appearance. It has numerous varieties, subvariants, and horticultural variants.

`Summer`

`15 cm`

Agave isthmensis 'Ouhi Raijin' f. variegata

Summer **10 cm**

The contrast between the young grass color and the white medium spots is beautiful. Spotted variants are more sensitive to direct summer sunlight so keep in semi-shade.

Agave hyb. seemannianax isthmensis

Summer **10 cm**

The overall form seems to be inherited from Seemanniana, while the spikes are inherited from isthmensis.

Agave kerchovei 'Huajuapan Red'

Summer **12 cm**

A horticultural variant of Agave kerchovei. Its red color is rare for agaves.

Agave lophantha 'Quadricolor'

Summer **10 cm**

It has a beautiful layering of colors: the dark green color of its linear patterns, the cream color of its spots, and reddish brown color of its spines.

Agave macroacantha 'Little Penguin'

Summer **10 cm**

A garden variety of macroacantha characterized by long, sharp spines on the tips of its leaves.

Agave ocahui

Summer **10 cm**

It has long and thin leaves with reddish-brown edges and spines. This is another example of a simple and beautiful agave.

Agave potatorum

Summer **13 cm**

Beautiful wavy rosette shape. It has many varieties and subvariants and it's also used as a parent in many hybrids.

Agave potatorum 'Cameron Blue'

Summer **13 cm**

Impressive reddish-brown long spines and well-defined shape. The "growth marks" of the agave are clearly visible in the photo.

Agave potatorum 'Cubic'

Summer **15 cm**

A monstrous variant of Agave potatorum. The ridges on the leaf backs create angles that add dimension to this plant, making it one of the most unique-looking succulents.

Agave potatorum *'Kisshoukan'* f. variegata

Summer **21 cm**

Kisshoukan can have many various speckle patterns, in this case the focus is placed on the ornamental border around the leaves. The contrast with the reddish-brown nails is gorgeous.

Agave pygmaea *'Dragon Toes'*

Summer **10 cm**

This variety is characterized by its white powdery leaves and the sharp serrated teeth that look like dragon claws.

Agave salmiana ssp. crassispina

Summer **10 cm**

The serrations are wide apart, as are the growth marks on the leaves.

Agave shrevei ssp. magna

Summer **10 cm**

A large agave variant. If planted in the ground, it can grow up to over 6–7'/2m in height, giving it a powerful appearance.

Agave stricta

Summer **10 cm**

It has thin, soft leaves spread in a radial pattern. Also known as Hedgehog Agave, its leaves ultimately grow in a rosette formation and can produce a sizable colony of offshoots.

Agave titanota

Summer **10 cm**

It has long, sharp spines, the strongest of any agave in fact. The spines are brown at first but turn white as they grow.

Agave victoriae-reginae

Summer **12 cm**

The ridges and edges of its leaves are white, giving it a striking look. It often produces plenty of offspring in clusters.

Agave wocomahi

Summer **10 cm**

It can grow to over 6–7'/2m when planted in the ground. It is quite resistant to cold weather and can survive mild winter outdoors.

Agave xylonacantha

Summer **10 cm**

When it grows, the edges of the leaves, including the spines, become covered with white fine hair.

Albuca
Asparagaceae genus

Place of Origin: Southern Africa **Growth Difficulty:** 3/3
Type: Spring-Fall **Watering:** between fall and spring, water generously when the soil is dry. During summer, water once a month just enough to moisten the surface of the soil.

Characteristics & Tips for Cultivation
A bulbous onion-like plant that grows between fall and spring. It really likes to be in good sunlight, so give it plenty of exposure. During the dormancy of most varieties in summer, the parts that are above the ground wither and only the bulbs are left. Keep them almost without water during summer and only resume watering in fall once the leaves start to grow again.

Albuca humilis

The thin leaves grow from onion-like bulbs. This variety is resistant to both heat and cold and it doesn't lose foliage during summer. It grows flowers in spring.

Spring-Fall **11 cm**

Ornithogalum hispidum

It has soft hairy leaves and grows white flowers in early summer. After flowering, it goes dormant and begins growing leaves again in fall.

Spring-Fall **11 cm**

Ornithogalum
Asparagaceae genus

Place of Origin: Southern Africa **Growth Difficulty:** 2/3
Type: Spring-Fall **Watering:** Water generously when the soil is dry between fall and spring. During summer, water once a month just enough to moisten the surface of the soil.

Characteristics & Tips for Cultivation
This bulbous plant has unique foliage, with both slender leaves and more cylindrical leaves. They should generally be planted in fall, but some varieties may vary. Begin watering when the leaves start to grow in fall. During dormancy in summer, keep the plant in well-ventilated half-shade with reduced watering.

Sansevieria
Asparagaceae genus

Place of Origin: Africa
Growth Difficulty: 3/3 **Type:** Summer
Watering: Water generously when the soil is dry, from spring to fall. During winter water very little and only once a month.

Characteristics & Tips for Cultivation
They have beautiful foliage with red edges or speckled leaves. Grow them outdoors in full sun from spring to fall. Although their native habitat is arid, they are relatively resistant of high humidity. It is sensitive to cold however and should be moved indoors in good sunlight when temperatures fall below 50°F/10°C.

Sansevieria boncellensis

It has a unique form that grows alternately to the left and right spreading out in a fan shape, giving it a mysterious presence. Weak to cold weather.

Summer **10 cm**

Drimiopsis
Asparagaceae genus

Place of Origin: Southern Africa **Growth Difficulty:** 3/3
Type: Summer **Watering:** Water generously when the soil is dry.

Drimiopsis maculata

In early summer, the plant grows flower stalks and blossoms with small white flowers (growing in a raceme). As temperatures drop, the leaves fall and emerge again in the following spring.

`Summer` `8 cm`

Characteristics & Tips for Cultivation
They used to be categorized under the Hyacinthaceae family, a different genus of bulbous plant. From spring to fall, give it plenty of water and expose them to plenty of sun. As temperatures drop, watering should be reduced gradually, and once all the leaves fall off, stop watering altogether.

Bowiea volubilis

It has jade green bulbs under a thin brown skin. When the vines turn brown and begin to wither and fall, gradually reduce the amount of watering, and once all leaves have fallen, stop watering altogether.

`Summer` `11 cm`

Bowiea
Asparagaceae genus

Place of Origin: Southern Africa
Growth Difficulty: 2/3
Type: Summer, Winter **Watering:** For summer types: From spring to fall, water generously when the soil is dry. For winter types: From fall to spring, water generously when the soil is dry.

Characteristics & Tips for Cultivation
One of the many tuberous root varieties (caudex), which grows thick roots and stems to store plenty of water and nutrients. During the growing season, they grow vines from their tuberous roots which produce new leaves and small white flowers. They are easy-to-grow plants but note that there are both summer and winter types.

Ledebouria
Asparagaceae genus

Place of Origin: Southern Africa **Growth Difficulty:** 3/3
Type: Summer **Watering:** From spring to fall, water generously when the soil is dry. Once all their leaves have fallen, stop watering altogether until they begin re-emerging in the next spring.

Ledebouria socialis 'Violacea'

The irregular pattern on its leaves is striking. In early summer, it grows flowers in lily-like racemes.

`Summer` `10 cm`

Characteristics & Tips for Cultivation
They can be considered bulbous plants. From spring to fall, water generously and keep in a good sunlight. As temperatures drop, watering should be reduced gradually, and once all the leaves fall off, stop watering altogether. Although they are relatively resistant to cold weather, it is best to keep them indoors during the winter.

Pachypodium
Asparagaceae genus

Place of Origin: Madagascar, Africa
Growth Difficulty: 1/3
Type: Summer
Watering: From spring to fall, water generously a few days after the soil dries out. Gradually reduce watering as their foliage falls. Once all their leaves have fallen, stop watering entirely until they begin re-emerging the next spring.

Characteristics One of the most popular caudex families. They are tuberous plants with enlarged stems. The stems can be cylindrical or flattened and spread out, making them the favorite genus of many succulent enthusiasts. Be aware that growing tips vary by variety.

Tips for Cultivation Even after growing vigorously for many years, they can easily wither and die. This is mainly caused by overwatering and excessive exposure to strong direct sunlight. Generally, you want to grow them in a well-ventilated environment with plenty of sunlight, but take special care against rain in the rainy season and protect them from direct sunlight in midsummer.

Pachypodium brevicaule   `Summer`

It's a very popular variety because of its unique flat and horizontal tuber. It naturally grows on rocky mountains at altitudes of 1,400 to 2,000 meters and grows in very dry rock crevices. Its main characteristic is that it grows extremely slowly. It's really weak to high summertime heat and humidity, and cold winter temperatures. It requires special care during rainy periods through the summer. Use fans or similar to prevent too much moisture from accumulating in the plant.

`8 cm` 2 years old

`9 cm` 5 to 10 years old

`20 cm` After a few years, the plant has gown to this size

It grows bright yellow flowers.

Pachypodium rosulatum var. gracilius   `Summer`

The name Pachypodium is a combination of the Greek words pachy (thick/fat) and podi (foot). The large, enlarged bulbs looks like "fat feet." It has yellow flowers. The key to growing a healthy gracilius that will survive for a long time is careful, moderate watering. It's also important to keep it well-ventilated.

`8 cm` 2 to 3 years old
The trunk still has a normal size.

`10 cm` A few decades old
The trunk starts growing into a round shape.

A plant that was picked from the mountains in Madagascar, where it grows naturally, and imported to Japan. It has been planted in culture soil so now we wait for its roots to emerge.

Pachypodium bispinosum

Summer **8 cm**

The ends of the branches contain spikes which appear to have evolved from stipules. It grows pretty bell-shaped, pale pink flowers in summer.

Pachypodium geayi

Summer **14 cm**

Characterized by sharp spines and faint hairs on the surface of its leaves. It is robust and easy to grow, although susceptible to cold.

Pachypodium horombense

Summer **18 cm**

The large plant in the photo is several decades old, and the small one is two years old. The roots are thin, so it should be watered only once a month during the dormant season, even in winter.

Pachypodium lamerei

Summer **10 cm**

Similar to Pach. Geayi but its leaves do not have hairs. It is robust and easy to grow.

Pachypodium namaquanum

Summer **8 cm**

It is popular for its thick, bottle-like trunk and wavy velvety hairs. It's also known for being somewhat difficult to grow.

Pachypodium rosulatum

Summer **14 cm**

The base variant of Pachypodium rosulatum. It grows yellow flowers. It has many varieties and subvarieties.

Pachypodium rosulatum var. eburneum

Summer **18 cm**

Rosulatum variants vary in the color of their flowers. eburneum has white flowers.

Pachypodium rosulatum var. cactipes

Summer **10 cm**

One of the variants of Pachypodium rosulatum, which has a reddish skin compared to the other variants. It grows yellow flowers.

Pachypodium succulentum

Summer **20 cm**

It's very similar to Pach. bispinosum, the only distinguishing feature being their flowers. Each flower petal has deep cuts that make them appear voluminous.

Sinningia
Gesneriaceae genus

Place of Origin: Africa, Central-South America
Growth Difficulty: 2/3 **Type:** Summer **Watering:** From spring to fall, water generously when the soil is dry. When the leaves start to fall, gradually reduce watering and once all leaves have fallen, stop watering altogether until new leaves emerge.

Characteristics They have thick stems made of round, flat tubers. The stem and leaves are covered with soft, thin hairs. The brightly colored tubular flowers have evolved due to hummingbirds being their main pollinators. Their leaves fall during their dormancy in winter and new ones emerge in the spring.

Tips for Cultivation They are weak to strong direct sunlight in midsummer (it is best to use shade nets to create a half-shaded area), but in general they enjoy full sunlight. Should be exposed to sunlight as much as possible from spring to fall, from when new shoots emerge until the leaves fall off. In winter, move indoors to a sunny area.

Sinningia 'Florianopolis'

The underside of its mint-like leaves is covered with white hairs. As it gets older, the tuber and its leaves grow stronger and larger.

Summer

8 cm

Sinningia leucotricha

The dense hairs on the stem and leaves are velvety. When the tubular red flowers bloom, the color contrast is truly beautiful. The plant in the photo is about 4 years old.

Summer

10 cm

Othonna
Asteraceae genus

Place of Origin: Africa, Central-South America
Growth Difficulty: 2/3 **Type:** Winter, but close to Spring-Fall
Watering: From spring to fall, water generously when the soil is dry. When the leaves start to fall, gradually reduce watering and once all leaves have fallen, stop watering altogether until new leaves emerge.

Characteristics Native mainly to southern Africa. It is a thick-stemmed caudex with a wide variety of attractive shapes. It grows long flower stalks that bloom from fall to winter.

Tips for Cultivation The thick stems and roots of these caudex variants are mostly submerged underground. It is best to keep them out of direct sunlight for long periods of time. During the dormant season, it would be ideal to stop watering altogether, but since many varieties of Othonna have thin roots, a little water should be given to the plants once a month.

Othonna clavifolia

Long, plump, and slender leaves emerge from its thick tubers. In its native habitat, it is almost spherical, but in the Japanese conditions, it grows in more irregular shapes.

Winter **9 cm**

Othonna furcata

Furcata means "branched" in Latin. It is characterized by its branching shape. Watering should be quite moderate all year round.

Winter **12 cm**

Sarcocaulon
Geraniaceae genus

Place of Origin: Southern Africa, Namibia
Growth Difficulty: 2/3 **Type:** Winter, but close to Spring-Fall
Watering: From spring to fall, water generously when the soil is dry. When the leaves start to fall, gradually reduce watering and once all leaves have fallen, stop watering altogether until new leaves emerge.

Characteristics The thick, shiny skin protects them from sandstorms, drought, and strong sunlight in their native habitat. The dead stems burn well and were once used by natives for bonfires and kindling, hence their English nickname "bushman's candle."

Tips for Cultivation They are native to desert regions. Keep in a well-ventilated location with direct sunlight in spring, fall, and early winter to let it grow nicely. In midsummer, use shade nets or keep in half-shade. In winter, it can be grown outdoors except in cold or snowy regions.

Sarcocaulon patersonii

Spring-Fall   **12 cm**

The appearance of small leaves growing from tough branches covered in spines and delicate flowers is quite attractive.

Portulaca
Portulacaceae genus

Place of Origin: Central-South America, etc.
Growth Difficulty: 3/3 **Type:** Summer **Watering:** From spring to fall, water generously when the soil is dry, moderately in winter.

Characteristics & Tips for Cultivation
Some of their variants produce small tuberous roots underground. They grow well in sunny, well-ventilated places. They are weak to cold, so move indoors in a well-lit place when temperatures fall below 41°F/5°C. Note: Not all Portulaca have the appearance of succulents. The popular garden annual Moss Rose Purlane is also a Portulaca (Portulaca grandiflora).

Portulaca molokiensis

Native to Hawaii. It is characterized by its alternating round leaves. It is sensitive to cold so move it indoors during winter and reduce watering.

Summer   **11 cm**

Portulaca werdermannii

Native to Brazil. The entire plant is covered in white hairs, and its flowers reside at the tips of the "branches," giving this plant a unique appearance. The flowers bloom for only a portion of the day, but bloom repeatedly from May to October.

Summer   **9 cm**

Avonia
Portulacaceae genus

Place of Origin: Africa **Growth Difficulty:** 2/3
Type: Winter, but close to Spring-Fall
Watering: From spring to fall, water generously when the soil is completely dry. Between the rainy season and summer, move to a well-ventilated spot in half-shade, with minimal watering (about once a month).

Characteristics & Tips for Cultivation
Their leaves are covered in stipules that look like fish scales. Because they are native to the extremely arid regions of Africa, they are very susceptible to high humidity. Should be kept in a sunny and well-ventilated places all year round and kept dry. Their tuberous roots grow slowly, only a few millimeters per year.

Its flowers open only a few hours before dusk on sunny evenings, during early summer. Its growth is slow, the one in the photograph is about 10 years old

`Winter` `10 cm`

Operculicarya pachypus

Younger plants have smaller roots that will grow into large tubers as the years go by. It is considered the king of the caudex family and is a very popular variety.

`Summer` `12 cm`

Operculicarya
Anacardiaceae genus

Place of Origin: Madagascar and Comoro Islands only.
Growth Difficulty: 2/3 **Type:** Summer **Watering:** From spring to fall, water generously when the soil is dry. When the leaves start to fall, gradually reduce watering and once all leaves have fallen, stop watering altogether until new leaves emerge.

Characteristics & Tips for Cultivation
Their trunk grows thicker and sturdier with age, giving it the appearance of a giant miniature tree. It grows slowly. Keep in a sunny location throughout the year. Even during its dormancy in winter, it should be exposed to the sun as much as possible because photosynthesis is carried out by chlorophyll under its skin.

Fockea
Apocynaceae Genus

Place of Origin: Southern Africa **Growth Difficulty:** 3/3
Type: Summer **Watering:** From spring to fall, water generously when the soil is dry. When the leaves start to fall, gradually reduce watering and once all leaves have fallen, stop watering altogether until new leaves emerge.

Characteristics & Tips for Cultivation
Rich in water and nutrients, the tuberous roots of some species are collected as an important food source by indigenous people living in arid regions. Moderate watering is essential as excessive watering may lead to rotting, even during its growing season. Keep in a sunny and well-ventilated spot.

Fockea edulis

It has protuberances on the surface of the tuberous root. It is sensitive to cold and should be moved indoors when the temperature drops below 59°F /15°C.

`Summer` `13 cm`

Dorstenia
Moraceae Genus

Place of Origin: Tropical regions in Africa, America and India
Growth Difficulty: 3/3 **Type:** Summer **Watering:** From spring to fall, water generously when the soil is dry. Reduce watering almost entirely during winter, giving only a small amount of water once a month.

Characteristics & Tips for Cultivation
In their native habitat they have both large and small tree varieties. It is highly adaptable to its environment and easy to grow. Many varieties are self-fruiting, and when their fruits are ripe, they pop and release seeds. In cold climates, they should be moved indoors during winter.

Dorstenia foetida

This variety produces unusually shaped flowers in summer, which self-pollinate and produce seeds that explode when the fruit is ripe enough. It's a variety that's full of life energy.

Summer **10 cm**

Stephania venosa

Its leaves fall during winter, but it grows vines from its tough tuberous roots at a very fast rate in summer.

Summer **18 cm**

Stephania
Menispermaceae Genus

Place of Origin: South-east Asia and islands in the pacific ocean.
Growth Difficulty: 3/3 **Type:** Summer **Watering:** From spring to fall, water generously when the soil is completely dry. Stop watering altogether in winter.

Characteristics & Tips for Cultivation
Being native to dark tropical rainforests, it prefers low light. Use a shade net to keep it in half-shade. Be especially careful not to expose the tuberous root to strong direct sunlight. When the temperatures fall below 41°F/5°C, move it indoors and stop watering altogether.

Alluaudia
Didiereaceae Genus

Place of Origin: Madagascar **Growth Difficulty:** 3/3
Type: Summer **Watering:** In summer, water generously when the soil is completely dry. When temperatures lower and the leaves start to fall, gradually reduce watering. Stop watering entirely during winter.

Characteristics & Tips for Cultivation
Native to Madagascar. Characterized by sharp spines growing from the trunk and branches. Can tolerate high temperatures and direct sunlight, but it is not cold hardy, so move it indoors in full sun when temperatures fall below 50°F/10°C.

Alluaudia procera

A spiny shrub with rounded leaves growing parallel to the soil. Each year new leaves "reuse" the spaces left by fallen leaves.

Summer **8 cm**

Adenia

Passifloraceae genus

Place of Origin: Tropical regions in Africa, Madagascar and Asia.
Growth Difficulty: 2/3 **Type:** Summer **Watering:** From spring to fall, water generously when the soil is completely dry. As the leaves begin to fall, gradually reduce watering. Stop watering entirely while it doesn't have any leaves.

Characteristics & Tips for Cultivation

It has both vine-like growing variants and others that grow in cylindrical stems from the ground. Vines should be pruned when they grow too long. Their native habitats vary from dry wastelands deep forests, so be aware that the optimal growing conditions may differ depending on the species.

Adenia glauca

If it grows into a long, slender tree, it can be cut at a certain length to give it a rounded caudex-like form.

Summer **10 cm**

Dioscorea elephantipes

It has heart-shaped leaves and rugged tuberous roots with gaps between them. The cracks become deeper and more tortoise-shell-patterned with age.

Summer **12 cm**

Dioscorea

Dioscoreaceae Genus

Place of Origin: Tropical and subtropical regions around the world
Growth Difficulty: 2/3 **Type:** Winter, but close to Spring-Fall
Watering: From the end of summer to the beginning of spring, water generously when the soil is dry. Drastically reduce watering during its dormant months.

Characteristics & Tips for Cultivation

Most Dioscorea varieties are edible and some are grown for horticultural purposes. They are native to dry wastelands and savannas. Their growth cycles tend to be shifted and generally have a pattern that about 1 month earlier than winter type succulents. They go dormant between mid- late spring to the end of the rainy season (June-July). New shoots begin to emerge after the rainy season.

Pseudolilthos

Apocynaceae Genus

Place of Origin: Central Africa, Arabian peninsula.
Growth Difficulty: 1/3 **Type:** Summer **Watering:** From spring to fall, water generously a few days after the soil dries out. As the leaves begin to fall, gradually reduce watering. Stop watering entirely while it doesn't have any leaves.

Characteristics & Tips for Cultivation

A rare genus with only about seven varieties known, native to eastern Africa and the Middle East. They are basically spherical but vary in surface details from species to species. They are sensitive to strong direct sunlight, cold weather, and high humidity. Keep them in well-ventilated location in half-shade and away from rain.

Pseudolithos migiurtinus

Ultimately the surface has a patterned texture, almost brain-like in appearance. This species is native to extremely arid areas, so it is especially important to keep it well-ventilated to avoid moisture.

Summer **12 cm**

Anacampseros

Portulacaceae Genus

Place of Origin: Southern Africa, Mexico
Growth Difficulty: 3/3 **Type:** Spring-Fall
Watering: From spring to fall, water generously when the soil dries out. Only water around once per month in mid-winter and midsummer.

Characteristics They grow in a variety of unique shapes, including some with small fleshy leaves and others with snake-like stems. They grow slowly but are hardy and easy to grow. They grow plenty of seeds, making it a good introduction for people who want to try sowing succulent seeds.

Tips for Cultivation Place them in a sunny, well-ventilated location. They do not tolerate high temperatures and humidity in midsummer, so use shade nets in summer to control their exposure to sunlight. In winter, when the temperature falls below 41°F/5°C, move indoors to a sunny spot.

Anacampseros arachnoides

Spring-Fall   8 cm

It has deep purple leaves surrounded by white threads that look like spider silk. New offspring emerges in clusters. It grows purple flowers in early summer.

Anacampseros baeseckei var. crinite

Spring-Fall   7 cm

It grows flowers in summer and produces seeds, which can be collected and planted. Also constantly grows new offspring on its own.

Anacampseros rufescens f. variegata

Spring-Fall   8 cm

It's a speckled variety of anacampseros rufescens. It's easy to grow from seeds and grows many pink flowers in early summer.

Senecio
Asteraceae Genus

Place of Origin: Africa, India, Mexico, and other arid regions. **Growth Difficulty:** 3/3 **Type:** Mainly Spring-Fall. Depending on the variety, their growth cycle may be closer to winter types or closer to summer types. Their dormancy period also varies from variant to variant. **Watering:** From spring to fall, water generously when the soil dries out. Also water a few times a month during the dormant season.

Characteristics There are about 2,000 species of Senecio in the world, but only about 80 are classified as succulent plants. There are many varieties with unusual shapes, for example some grow small-round leaves and others grow arrow-shaped leaves. They also grow flowers in a wide variety of colors, including red, yellow, purple, and white.

Tips for Cultivation They go dormant in either summer or winter depending on the variety, but regardless of dormancy periods, all Senecio varieties have their growth periods in spring and fall. Regulate temperature and sunlight according to the variety. While they are also weak to high humidity, their thin roots are also susceptible to extreme drought, so even during their dormant seasons, water a small amount a few times a month.

Senecio articulatus

It has a curious shape that looks like many cucumbers attached to each other. It goes dormant in summer, so keep it in well-ventilated half-shade and water it sparingly.

Spring-Fall **10 cm**

Senecio crassissimus

It has oval leaves with faint white powder and purple-red edges. The flowers it grows in spring are typical of Asteraceae.

Spring-Fall **8 cm**

Senecio rowleyanus

The round, bell-like leaves like to hang from pots and work well in mixed arrangements. It should be kept in semi-shade in summer.

Spring-Fall **10 cm**

Senecio haworthii

It has a beautiful form covered with thin white hairs. It's susceptible to high humidity, so it requires good ventilation and constant trimming. It goes dormant in summer.

Spring-Fall **8 cm**

Senecio kleinia

It has a unique stem pattern. In the Canary Islands, where this plant is native, some legends say that touching its stem brings happiness and fortune. It goes dormant in summer.

Spring-Fall   **10 cm**

Senecio kleiniiformis "Masai's Arrow-heads" in Japanese

As its name tells us, the leaves look like arrowheads. It is susceptible to high temperatures and humidity in summer and somewhat resistant to cold in winter. Move indoors when temperatures fall below 32°F/0°C.

Spring-Fall   **8 cm**

Senecio saginatus

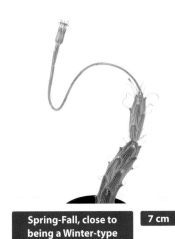

It has a unique surface pattern with branching starting from the stem tips all over. It grows large tuberous roots underground.

Spring-Fall, close to being a Winter-type   **7 cm**

Senecio scaposus var. *'Hougetsu'*

A variant of scaposus with flattened leaf tips. Be careful to not overwater during the growing season.

Spring-Fall, close to being a Winter-type   **10 cm**

Senecio serpens

Keep in full sun in spring and fall, shade in summer. Keep it indoors in winter but move it outside in the sun on warm days.

Spring-Fall   **8 cm**

Senecio stapeliformis

A variety with only long, thin stems growing above the surface, a common shape in many Senecio varieties. It should be placed in a large pot because it grows tuberous roots below the soil surface.

Spring-Fall   **7 cm**

Orbea

Apocynaceae Genus

Place of Origin: Africa
Growth Difficulty: 2/3
Type: Summer **Watering:** From spring to fall, water generously when the soil completely dries out. Gradually reduce watering as temperatures fall. Stop watering altogether when temperatures fall under 50°F/10°C. Gradually resume watering when the flowers begin to grow.

Characteristics Formerly categorized as Asclepiadaceae. They are characterized by thick stems lined with spiny protuberances. They grow starfish shaped flowers that bloom directly from the stem. Many of the flowers of this family emit an unpleasant odor, which encourages pollination by flies.

Tips for Cultivation From spring to fall, place outdoors in a sunny, well-ventilated location away from rain. It's weak to direct sunlight in midsummer Avoid high humidity. In winter, when the temperature drops below 41°F/5°C, move indoors in a bright environment.

Orbea caudata

Summer | 8 cm

The plant is rather like a miniature thorn grove, and in keeping with that form, its yellow flowers are like sharply-pointed stars. It has a strong odor.

Orbea namaquensis

Summer | 8 cm

Anywhere from 1–4 fleshy, mottled flowers are produced in succession. If you look at it closely, you can see minute hairs on the flower.

Orbea semitubiflora

Summer | 8 cm

The purple-specked stems are covered in spines. Its star-shaped flowers have a deep red color and a strong scent.

Orbea semota var. lutea

Summer | 8 cm

The yellow star-fish-shaped flower is both textured and hairy . The flowers bloom from the base of its short stems.

An unforgettable look: **Flowers of the Orbea species**

What are Orbea?

Native to Southern Africa and parts of Arabia, this genus has been reclassified several times since its first description in 1812. It derives its name from the raised *orbis* (circle) at the center of most of these species. They are pollinated by various species of fly, which are attracted by both the odor (this species is often called "carrion flower") and the movement of the hairs that some species have at the edge of their centers. In the Orbea genus, spines/thorns take the place of leaves. In combination with the unusual flowers (in both look and smell), this makes for a very "intense-looking" plant that collectors prize.

hislopii

insigniflora

macrocarpa

zebrina

'Korat Crimson'

oculata

lutea

panculata

crenulata

namaquensis

'Pink Eye'

Huernia

Apocynaceae Genus

Place of Origin: Africa, Arabian peninsula.
Growth Difficulty: 2/3
Type: Summer
Watering: From spring to fall, water generously when the soil in the pot is completely dry. Gradually reduce the amount of water and stop watering when the temperatures drop below 50°F/10°C. Gradually resume watering gradually around mid to end of spring.

Characteristics Formerly a member of the Asclepiadaceae. This family has over sixty different species growing their native regions. Their jagged stems have spiny protuberances and spikes, and star-shaped or starfish-shaped flowers abruptly bloom from the stems. As with the Orbea genus, its flowers have a carrion-like odor that attracts pollinator flies.

Tips for Cultivation From spring to fall, place it outdoors in a sunny, well-ventilated location that can't be hit by rain. They are sensitive to direct sunlight, so place under cover or use a shade net. Take precautions against high humidity as well. In winter, when the temperatures fall below 41°F/5°C, move them indoors in full sun.

Huernia brevirostris

Huernia hislopii

As shown here, the stems can tend to grow in irregular clumps. Its striking flowers are off-white with red spots.

Summer   **8 cm**

Summer   **10 cm**

It grows as a dense group of stems, which are about 2"/5cm in height. It has five-petaled, star-shaped flowers, yellow in color with small dots, that bloom in summer.

Huernia insigniflora

Stems grow in dense clumps and may be inclined to tilt. Its yellow flowers have a fleshy red ring at the center.

Summer   **8 cm**

Huernia 'Korat Crimson'

Summer **8 cm**

Stems have a pattern of rounded spots. The flowers appear drenched in their deep red color.

Huernia 'Korat Star'

Summer **8 cm**

Stems have firm spikes. The flowers are a pale creamy yellow, red-dotted. The red color becomes increasingly concentrated toward the center.

Huernia macrocarpa

Summer **9 cm**

The spines on its stem are more supple and less sharp, as they evolved from leaves. Reddish-purple flowers bloom from the base of the stems.

Huernia oculata

Summer **8 cm**

The thinness of the stems and the overall growth pattern can make it look like it's collapsing. It grows yellow, red-dotted flowers.

Huernia pillansii

The stems are covered with thin, soft spines. It grows yellow flowers with fine red dots, which can dominate, and thin spines along the petal edges.

Summer
11 cm

Huernia 'Pink Eye'

Summer **8 cm**

The flowers have a coral pink gradient and the pattern of fine dots. The color intensity varies from flower to flower.

Huernia zebrina

Summer **8 cm**

It's native to a wide variety of regions and environments and has many variations of flowers. The flower petals of all subvariants and variants in the zebrina variety have a zebra-stripe pattern. The center of their flowers may have patterns or dots instead. Colors and patterns vary among subspecies and variants.

Stapelia
Apocynaceae Genus

Place of Origin: Southern Africa, Tropical Asia, Central/Southern America
Growth Difficulty: 2/3
Type: Summer
Watering: From spring to fall, water generously when the soil in the pot is completely dry. Gradually reduce the amount of water and stop watering altogether when temperatures drop below 50°F/10°C. Resume watering gradually around mid to end of spring.

Characteristics Formerly a member of the Asclepiad-aceae. Found in arid environments such as wastelands and rocky mountains in Africa and tropical Asia. Produces flowers with a strong odor.

Tips for Cultivation From spring to fall, keep outdoors in a sunny, well-ventilated, rainproof location. Also take measures against humidity. In winter, when the temperatures fall below 41°F/5°C, move indoors in full sun.

Stapelia divaricata

The jagged stems are a typical trait of stapelia. Its flowers are starfish-shaped and speckled with a red pattern on a white background.

`Summer` `8 cm`

Stapelia grandiflora

It grows over 4'/10cm in diameter. Its textured, hairy flowers can vary from a coral pink to a deep red-purple, or may have a yellow base with strong red edges--very high-impact,

`Summer` `8 cm`

Stapelia paniculata

Deep red flowers bloom from the base of its stems. The petals have small, similarly colored, snail-shaped protu-berances.

`Summer` `9 cm`

Stapelia schinzii

Its stems twist into the ground and it grows star-shaped, crimson-colored flowers. These can grow quite large relative to their stem size.

`Summer` `8 cm`

Caralluma
Apocynaceae Genus

Place of Origin: Africa, Arabian peninsula, India
Growth Difficulty: 2/3 **Type:** Summer **Watering:** From spring to fall, water generously when the soil in the pot is completely dry. Gradually reduce the amount of water and stop watering altogether when temperatures drop below 50°F/10°C. Resume watering gradually around mid to end of spring.

Characteristics & Tips for Cultivation
Their flowering is unique: with multiple flowers blooming in a cone shape at the tip of flower stems. Grow in a sunny and well-ventilated rainproof environment. In winter, they should receive almost no water and be kept in a warm room. The same basic tips for growing Asclepiadaceae apply to Stapelia.

Caralluma crenulata

Flowers grow in clusters. After blooming, they fold up and wither away. The creeping stems make this a good choice for a hanging plant.

`Summer` `8 cm`

Duvalia sulcata

Its flowers are crimson with a dark brown pattern on grayish-green stems. The petals are striped with red hairs on their edges.

`Summer` `8 cm`

Duvalia
Apocynaceae Genus

Place of Origin: Africa, Arabian peninsula.
Growth Difficulty: 2/3 **Type:** Summer **Watering:** From spring to fall, water generously when the soil in the pot is completely dry. Gradually reduce the amount of water and stop watering altogether when temperatures drop below 50°F/10°C. Resume watering gradually around mid to end of spring.

Characteristics & Tips for Cultivation
They can have two types of stems: some have spines, which is typical of the former Asclepiadaceae family, and the others have rounded stems. Both types have star or starfish-shaped flowers. The same basic tips for growing Asclepiadaceae apply to Duvalia.

Pilea
Urticaceae Genus

Place of Origin: Tropical regions around the world
Growth Difficulty: 1/3
Type: Summer **Watering:** From spring to summer, water generously when the soil in the pot is dry. During winter just barely wet the surface of the soil a few times a month.

Characteristics & Tips for Cultivation
There is a wide variety of species in the Pilea family, from herbaceous plants to shrubs. Many varieties are cultivated for their beautiful leaf patterns. They are highly resistant to heat but sensitive to cold, so when temperatures drop below 50°F/10°C, move them indoors in a well-lit environment.

Pilea serpyllacea 'Globosa'

This plant has petite round leaves and even smaller flowers. It works very well as an accent in mixed arrangements.

`Summer` `10 cm`

Ceropegia
Apocynaceae Genus

Place of Origin: Southern Africa, Madagascar, Tropical Asia
Growth Difficulty: 1/3
Type: Summer, Spring-Fall
Watering: Depends on growth type.

Characteristics Formerly members of the Asclepiadaceae family. Ceropegia can have very diverse shapes, with some with rod-shaped stems and others with vine-like stems emerging from their tuberous roots. Many of them grow to resemble bizarre-looking grass, giving it an unusual impression even among other former Asclepiadaceae varieties. They grow small gourd-shaped flowers.

Tips for Cultivation The same basic tips for growing Asclepiadaceae apply to Ceropegia. Most varieties with vine-like stems are spring-fall types. Summer types are sensitive to cold, so when temperatures drop below 50°F/10°C, move them indoors in a well-lit environment.

Ceropegia bosseri

It has a truly unusual, even bizarre appearance. The small leaves fall off shortly after growing. It grows gourd-shaped flowers in summer.

Summer　**12 cm**

Ceropegia cimiciodora

This species looks even more bizarre than bosseri. It has extremely small leaves, and grows in a single cylindrical shape without branching.

Summer　**8 cm**

Peperomia
Piperaceae Genus

Place of Origin: Central and Southern America, Africa, Asia
Growth Difficulty: 1/3
Type: Spring-Fall
Watering: In spring and fall, water generously when the soil in the pot is dry. Water in moderation in summer and winter.

Characteristics & Tips for Cultivation
They are small plants growing on trees and other plants in their native forests. More than 1,500 species are known, mainly from South America. Some of them have transparent windows. They are sensitive to direct sunlight in summer, high humidity, and cold in winter, so they require care and proper management in each season.

Peperomia 'Cactusville'

Leaves cluster densely on their stems. Keep away from strong direct sunlight to prevent leaf burn.

Spring-Fall　**8 cm**

Peperomia columella

A very small variety of Peperomia. The small leaves overlap like beads, and each stem is about 4"/10 cm tall.

Spring-Fall　**10 cm**

Dyckia
Bromeliaceae Genus

Place of Origin: Southern America, Africa
Growth Difficulty: 3/3
Type: Summer
Watering: From spring to fall, water generously when the soil in the pot is dry. Water moderately during dormancy in winter, about once a month with very little water.

Characteristics They have slender leaves with sharp spikes spreading in a radial pattern. It has many fans because of its well-defined foliage and chic coloring. In recent years, many new hybrids have been produced. They are hardy and easy to grow.

Tips for Cultivation Expose them to full sun from spring to fall, keeping them in a well-ventilated, sunny, rainproof location. When the temperature drops below 41°F/5°C, move them indoors in a bright environment.

Dyckia *'Brittle Star'*

Spring-Fall **9 cm**

The most popular variety among all Dyckia hybrids. It is very strong-featured, with a beautiful balance of deep purple leaves, white powdery pattern and thorny spines.

Dyckia *'Burgundy Ice'*

The deep purple and dark green colors blended together give the plant an austere look. The leaves have small spines. In summer produces stalks of bright orange flowers.

Summer **9 cm**

Dyckia *'Gran Marnier White Foliage'*

It has white, whiskery spines, and white powder covers the entire plant. A purple tint can be seen beneath the powder and on the undersides.

Summer **9 cm**

Tillandsia

Bromeliaceae Genus

Place of Origin: From southern North America to Central/South America.
Growth Difficulty: 2/3
Type: Summer
Watering: Use water mist to moisten the entire plant: every 2–3 days between spring and fall; every 7–10 days in winter.

Characteristics In their native habitat, they grow on tree branches, absorbing dew and rainwater through the leaves and roots. The leaves have hairs (called trichomes) on their surface to protect them from strong sunlight and to collect water. Tillandsia are divided into silver-leafed and green-leafed types according to their trichome density.

Tips for Cultivation The same basic tips for growing most succulents apply here too. The general temperature range for growing them outdoors is 50°F/10°C to 86°F/30°C. When the maximum temperature rises above 86°F/30°C, move them to a well-ventilated location in half-shade. When the minimum temperature falls below 50°F/10°C, move them indoors in a bright location.

Tillandsia brachycaulos

A green-leaved variety with few trichomes. It is sensitive to direct summer sunlight and prone to experiencing leaf burn, so it should be kept in half-shade during the summer.

Summer **15 cm**

Tillandsia bulbosa

A green-leaved variety. The bulbous base has white and purple lines of trichomes. It's very popular for its beautiful coloring.

Summer **15 cm**

Tillandsia capitata

A green-leaved variety. Many Tillandsia species have leaves that change color during the flowering period, and capitata is one of them.

Summer **15 cm**

Tillandsia caput-medusae

A silver-leafed variety. The base of the plant is bulging and has a vase-like shape. Its flower stalks emerge from between the wavy leaves and produce purple flowers.

Summer **20 cm**

Tillandsia *'Cotton Candy'*

Summer **17 cm**

A silver-leafed variety. Its flower stalks emerge from between the wavy leaves, producing peach-colored bracts, purple petals, and clusters of flowers.

Tillandsia fasciculate

Green leaf type. It grows up to nearly 32"/80cm in length. The leaves gradually spread horizontally in a radial pattern and take a water fountain shape.

Summer **25 cm**

Tillandsia fuchsii f. gracilis

Summer **14 cm**

A silver-leafed variety. It has delicate leaves that are only about 1mm in diameter. It grows a row of small, slender flowers that bloom from the center of the plant.

Tillandsia harrisii

Summer **18 cm**

A representative silver-leafed variety. It grows large flowers with orange bracts and purple petals.

Tillandsia ionantha

Summer **8 cm**

It has many variants and subspecies. For example, the variants in Guatemala have long, thin leaves and the variants in Mexico have short, meaty leaves.

Tillandsia juncifolia

Tillandsia juncifolia is a green-leafed species. The long, thin leaves are stylish. It looks very similar to the silver-leafed variety juncea.

Summer **25 cm**

Tillandsia kolbii

Summer **10 cm**

A silver-leafed variety. It is characterized by its long leaves all curving in the same direction. Its leaves turn red during the flowering season.

Tillandsia pseudobaileyi

Summer **18 cm**

A green-leafed variety. The leaves are thin but stiff, and each leaf grows in random directions. It has a unique form.

Tillandsia *'Tricolor'*

Summer **16 cm**

A green-leafed variety. It is hardy and easy to grow, but water can easily accumulate in the base of the plant, causing damage to the plant.

Mammillaria

Cactaceae Genus

Place of Origin: Western North America, South America, Caribbean Archipelago
Growth Difficulty: 3/3
Type: Summer
Watering: In spring and fall, water generously when the soil in the pot is dry. In midsummer, early spring, late fall, wait a few days after the soil dries out before watering. Water once a month in winter.

Characteristics The genus name comes from the Latin word meaning "wart." They are native to dry desert regions and enjoy strong sunlight, good ventilation, and dry soil. They have a wide variety of spines, from soft hairy types to hard prickly types. They produce brightly-colored flowers.

Tips for Cultivation Place in sunny, well-ventilated, rainproof locations. Being native to desert regions, which are hot during the day and cold at night, they are highly tolerant of heat and cold, but are weak to high humidity. Move them indoors in chilly environments during humid nights and keep them indoors in a bright environment over winter.

Mammillaria backebergiana

Its ivory-colored spines emerging from the stigmas and the bright corolla-shaped flowers are typical features of Mammillaria.

Summer **9 cm**

Mammillaria carmenae

The delicate spines that emerge from each wart are a characteristic feature of this variety. Its flowers may be pink or white.

Summer **7 cm**

Mammillaria elongata

They often blow their offspring away and grow in clusters. Characterized by gently curved, recurved spines. Their color varies from yellow to reddish brown. This species has many crested variants.

Summer **7 cm**

Mammillaria guelzowiana

A more spherically-shaped Mammillaria. Its white hairs look like cotton and it has red spines that curve like hooks. Its flowers Flowers range from bright pink to deep red and can be relatively large.

Summer **7 cm**

Mammillaria hahniana

Summer **9 cm**

It has a round body covered in white hairs. They should be kept dry, so water the soil around the plant to avoid wetting them.

Mammillaria hernandezii

Summer **7 cm**

Each wart has a stigma from which spines emerge. Its ovoid shape is another form that is typical of Mammillaria .

Mammillaria herrerae

Summer **7 cm**

It has a beautiful form created by its radial spines that emerge inward. In spring, it grows pink Corolla-shaped flowers.

Mammillaria marksiana

Summer **7 cm**

This variety is distinguished by its glossy green skin and the hairs that grow between the warts. It grows Yellow flowers in late winter.

Mammillaria schiedeana f. monstrosa

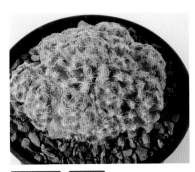

Summer **7 cm**

A petrified white variety of schiedeana. Its warts are densely arranged.

Mammillaria spinosissima 'Pico'

Summer **9 cm**

The warts on its glossy green skin grow arranged in a regular fashion. It grows pink Corolla-shaped flowers.

Mammillaria spinosissima

Summer **9 cm**

The corolla-shaped flowers are a characteristic feature in Mammillaria. The spikes have a lovely red-to-white color gradation.

Mammillaria gracilis

It looks very neat as if covered in lace fabric with flowers on top. It often produces seeds and grows in clusters.

Summer

7 cm

Astrophytum
Cactaceae Genus

Place of Origin: From Mexico to Western North America.
Growth Difficulty: 3/3
Type: Summer
Watering: In spring and fall, water generously when the soil in the pot is dry. In midsummer, early spring, late fall, wait a few days after the soil dries out before watering. Once a month in winter.

Characteristics The name is derived from the Greek words astro (star) and phyton (tree). They are popular cactus family since long ago; they have been cultivated and bred for over 100 years, with many hybrids. They are sensitive to strong direct sunlight, so they should be kept in shade during in summer.

Tips for Cultivation Place in a sunny, well-ventilated, rainproof location. They are native to arid regions with hot days and cool nights. Because of that they are highly tolerant of heat and cold but are weak high humidity. Move them indoors in chilly environments during humid nights and keep them indoors in a bright environment over winter.

Astrophytum asterias 'Super Kabuto'

An enhanced variety of 'Kabuto', which is characterized by its white hair-like dots. The dots in this variety are larger and denser than in the original 'Kabuto'.

Summer | **7 cm**

Astrophytum myriostigma var. nudum

Summer | **18 cm**

Astrophytum ornatum

It has sharp spines and sharp ridges. A powerful-looking variety; in its native habitat, it can grow over 39"/1m long and takes several years to flower.

Summer | **7 cm**

Nudum is just one of many varieties, subspecies, and hybrids of myriostig-mais. Instead of the characteristic white spots in myriostigma, it has a matte green skin with a check-like pattern and hairs on the ridges.

Gymnocalycium
Cactaceae Genus

Place of Origin: Argentina, Uruguay, Paraguay, Bolivia
Growth Difficulty: 3/3
Type: Summer
Watering: In spring and fall, water generously when the soil in the pot is dry. In midsummer, early spring, late fall, wait a few days after the soil dries out before watering. Water once a month in winter.

Characteristics Characterized by large spines and a variety of shapes. They blow new seeds from their stigmas. Their flowering season goes from spring to fall: their short flower stalks emerge from the stigma at the top, producing large pink, red or yellow flowers.

Tips for Cultivation Place in a sunny, well-ventilated, rainproof location. Because they are native to grassland areas, they are less resistant to strong sunlight compared to other cacti, so water them a little more frequently. Use shade nets in summer and move them indoors during winter.

Gymnocalycium anisitsii

Gymnocalycium saglionis

If you look closely at the color of the leaves, you can see a gradation of deep purple and grayish green. Its flowers bloom one after another from spring to fall.

Summer   7 cm

Gymnocalycium pflanzii ssp. Zegarrae

It has sharp, beautiful spikes that protrude from its round, firmer ridges. Its top produces lovely blush-colored flowers.

Summer   7 cm

Summer   7 cm

Similar to Zegarrae, but has more distinct ridges and longer spines.

Echinopsis
Cactaceae Genus

Place of Origin: South America
Growth Difficulty: 3/3 **Type:** Summer **Watering:** In spring and fall, water generously when the soil in the pot is dry. In midsummer, early spring, late fall, wait a few days after the soil dries out before watering. Water once a month in winter.

Characteristics Several hundred of their varieties are native to South America, from regions including Brazil and Argentina. Sometimes called the "hedgehog cactus," is all of its species produce vibrant flowers. It is hardy and easy to grow.

Tips for Cultivation Place in a sunny, well-ventilated, rainproof location. They are less resistant to strong sunlight compared to other cacti, water them a little more frequently. Use shade nets in summer and move them indoors during winter.

Echinopsis calochlora

It has a round shape with golden spines that give it a classic cactus appearance. It has to grow for many years before it can produce its large white flowers.

`Summer` `7 cm`

Echinopsis subdenudata

Not having any spines, the "naked" stigmas around the ridges are its charm points. It grows large white flowers that bloom before summer.

`Summer` `7 cm`

Turbinicarpus
Cactaceae Genus

Place of Origin: Mexico
Growth Difficulty: 3/3
Type: Summer
Watering: In spring and fall, water generously when the soil in the pot is dry. In midsummer, early spring, late fall, wait a few days after the soil dries out before watering. Water once a month in winter.

Characteristics Native only to Mexico, this genus only contains fifteen species which however have a wide variety of subspecies and variants. The shape of their spines can be straight or curly, depending on the variety. They grow large flowers that only bloom during the day. The flowers bloom from the very top of the plant.

Tips for Cultivation Place them in sunny, well-ventilated, rainproof locations. They are less resistant to strong sunlight compared to other cacti. Use shade nets in summer and move them indoors to a bright environment during winter.

Turbinicarpus krainzianus

It's characterized by its spines that look like an old man's beard. It grows lemon-yellow flowers that bloom in summer.

`Summer` `7 cm`

Turbinicarpus pseudopectinatus

The soft, inward-facing spines protect the plant from strong sunlight. It grows large, reddish-purple flowers in spring.

`Summer` `7 cm`

Tephrocactus / Thelocactus
Cactaceae Genus

Place of Origin: Argentina, Chile, Bolivia
Growth Difficulty: 3/3 **Type:** Summer
Watering: In spring and fall, water generously when the soil in the pot is dry. In midsummer, early spring, late fall, wait a few days after the soil dries out before watering. Water once a month in winter.

Characteristics There are fifteen species of Tephrocactus that have been isolated from Opuntia. They grow in clusters of spherical or oval shapes. They also have the ability to spread their seeds very far. There are more than ten species of Thelocactus that have been isolated from Echinocactus that are currently known; they grow either in a cylindrical or spherical shape and their flowers grow from the very top of the plants.

Tips for Cultivation Place in a sunny, well-ventilated, rainproof location. They are less resistant to strong sunlight compared to other cacti, water them a little more than other cacti. Use shade nets in summer and move them indoors during winter.

Tephrocactus geometricus

As it grows, it looks like a bunch of green spheres stacked on each other. It can turn red when exposed to plenty of sunlight.

Summer **11 cm**

Thelocactus macdowellii

At a glance, it looks like a Mammilaria (p. 156). Instead of having corolla-shaped flowers growing around it, its flowers grow at the very top of the plant. It self-pollinates and produces seeds.

Summer **7 cm**

Rhipsalis
Cactaceae Genus

Place of Origin: Tropical regions from southern North America to South America **Growth Difficulty:** 3/3 **Type:** Spring-Fall
Watering: They like high humidity but over-exposing them to moisture is not good. In spring and fall, water generously when the soil in the pot is dry. Barely water during winter (but if kept indoors, spray some water mist every now and then to keep them moist). In midsummer, early spring, late fall, wait a few days after the soil dries out before watering. Water once a month in winter.

Characteristics In nature, they grow on tall mountains by attaching their roots to other plants or rocks. They have characteristic bamboo-like joints on their stems, which start to droop down as they grow. They grow small cream or white colored flowers which bloom and self-pollinate to produce fruit. The fruit contains seeds.

Tips for Cultivation Being from tropical regions, they can survive highly humid environments, however, you should avoid letting them accumulate moisture. So, wait a few days after the soil has dried out before watering them again. When temperatures drop below 50°F/10°C, move them indoors to a bright environment. To cut and replant them, cut along their nodes.

Rhipsalis 'Britton and Rose'

The new shoots are reddish and full of spines, but as they mature they also turn green and most of their spines fall off.

Summer
11 cm

Rhipsalis pilocarpa

As it matures, the stems elongate and turn bright green. The fine spines lend a sugar-coated look to the stems.

Summer
7 cm

Rebutia

Cactaceae Genus

Place of Origin: Argentina, Bolivia
Growth Difficulty: 3/3
Type: Summer
Watering: In spring and fall, water generously when the soil in the pot is dry. In midsummer, early spring, late fall, wait a few days after the soil dries out before watering. Water once a month in winter.

Characteristics They naturally grow in the rock crevices in mountains at altitudes of 4000–12000 feet (1200–3600m) above sea level. They have warts that look similar to those of Mammillaria; however, their flowers are not corolla-shaped, but funnel-shaped, blooming from the base of the plants or from the sides of their warts. They are sensitive to strong direct sunlight, so keep them in shade during summer.

Tips for Cultivation Place in a sunny, well-ventilated, rainproof location. They are sensitive to direct sunlight and high humidity in summer, so use shade nets to protect them. In winter, when temperatures fall below 41°F/5°C, move them indoors in bright environments.

Rebutia minuscula var. aureiflora

It's characterized by the yellow flowers blooming at the base of the plant. Depending on timing, the flowers may grow in a shape surrounding the plant itself.

Summer   9 cm

Rebutia perplexa

A beautiful clumping cactus with profuse wisteria-colored blooms. These bloom in spring, opening when in direct sunlight.

Summer   9 cm

Lophophora

Cactaceae Genus

Place of Origin: Texas, Mexico
Growth Difficulty: 3/3 **Type:** Summer **Watering:** In spring and fall, water generously when the soil in the pot is dry. In midsummer, early spring, late fall, wait a few days after the soil dries out before watering. Water once a month in winter.

Characteristics There are only three known species in this small genus, but thanks to the succulent community, quite a few unique hybrids have been produced. They have no spines, and are believed to contain a poisonous chemical to protect them from predators. They have tuberous roots growing under the surface of the soil and short spherical stems.

Tips for Cultivation Place in a sunny, well-ventilated, rainproof location. They are sensitive to direct sunlight and high humidity in summer, so use shade nets to protect them. In winter, when temperatures fall below 41°F/5°C, move them indoors in bright environments.

Lophophora diffusa

This plant is hardy and easy to grow but be careful not to splash water on the hairs of its stigma. Pink to pinkish white flowers grow on top.

Summer   13 cm

Lophophora williamsii 'Caespitosa' f. variegata

This is a horticultural variant of Lophophora williamsii that can reproduce repeatedly. Williamsii, also called Peyote, is a hallucinogen, and is illegal in some parts of the world.

Summer   10 cm

Epithelantha
Cactaceae Genus

Place of Origin: South America **Growth Difficulty:** 3/3
Type: Summer **Watering:** In spring and fall, water generously when the soil in the pot is dry. In midsummer, early spring, late fall, wait a few days after the soil dries out before watering. Water once a month in winter.

Characteristics & Tips for Cultivation A small cactus that grows in the shade of rocks in desert areas. They are characterized by their whitish appearance caused by the stigma and fine spines that are attached to the stem. They grow really slowly, but many of their varieties grow in clusters. Clustered plants tend to get humid, so they should be taken care of with special attention to ventilation.

Eriosyce nidus

A beautiful variety with white spikes that grow longer as they ascend to the apex, and petals that look like a fountain.

Summer   9 cm

Sulcorebutia
Cactaceae Genus

Place of Origin: Madagascar and other islands **Growth Difficulty:** 3/3 **Type:** Spring-Fall **Watering:** In spring and fall, water generously when the soil in the pot is dry. In midsummer and winter reduce watering to only once a month or so.

Characteristics & Tips for Cultivation Since most of their varieties are native to arid regions at high elevations, they are spring and fall-type, unlike most other cacti. They are hardy and can tolerate relatively low temperatures. They can even survive outdoors over winter in regions where it doesn't snow. They are however weaker to high humidity, high temperatures and direct sunlight compared to other cacti and require care during summer.

Epithelantha micromeris ssp. bokei

Its fine white spines grow so densely that the surface of the stem can hardly be seen. It also has a variant that grows in clusters (see photo below).

Summer   7 cm

Eriosyce
Cactaceae Genus

Place of Origin: Argentina, Mexico, Bolivia **Growth Difficulty:** 3/3 **Type:** Summer, Spring-Fall **Watering:** In spring and fall, water generously when the soil in the pot is dry. In midsummer, early spring, late fall, wait a few days after the soil dries out before watering. Water once a month in winter.

Characteristics & Tips for Cultivation Formerly included in the Neoporteria genus and later in the Islaya genus, they are now categorized as Eriosyce. They are native to arid regions which vary in altitude from sea level to about 9800'/3000m. Flowers are apexed. Because of the wide difference in altitude between their habitats, the number of ridges and spines is also very varied depending on the species. They grow flowers that bloom on their apex (tallest part of the plant).

Sulcorebutia rauschii

The color of its stems' skin varies from reddish purple to green. It is a popular variety because of its clumpy and cluttered appearance.

Summer

9 cm

Stenocactus
Cactaceae Genus

Place of Origin: Mexico **Growth Difficulty:** 3/3
Type: Summer, Spring-Fall **Watering:** In spring and fall, water generously when the soil in the pot is dry. In midsummer, early spring, late fall, wait a few days after the soil dries out before watering. Water once a month in winter.

Characteristics & Tips for Cultivation They grow exclusively in Mexico but at altitudes varying from sea level to 9000'/2800m, They grow small flowers that bloom on their apex. They don't self-pollinate and can only be bred by planting their fruits. Keep in shade during summer. They are relatively strong against cold but move them indoors if the temperatures fall below 41°F/5°C.

Stenocactus multicostatus

It has a unique form with up to 100 ridges. It takes a long time to grow, taking about 4 to 5 years to go from seedling to its first bloom.

`Spring-Fall` `9 cm`

Parodia haselbergii ssp. haselbergii

Characterized by its white stigmas and white spines. It grows red flowers in spring. Keep away from direct sunlight and take measures against high temperatures and humidity in summer.

`Summer` `9 cm`

Parodia
Cactaceae Genus

Place of Origin: South America **Growth Difficulty:** 3/3
Type: Summer, Spring-Fall **Watering:** In spring and fall, water generously when the soil in the pot is dry. In midsummer, early spring, late fall, wait a few days after the soil dries out before watering. Water once a month in winter.

Characteristics & Tips for Cultivation They have uneven and well-defined ridges, their spines can be straight or curved, and their flowers can be yellow, white, or brown in color. They grow in clusters but do not blow their offspring far. Flowers are self-pollinated and produce fruit and seeds.

Ferocactus
Cactaceae Genus

Place of Origin: From southern North America to Mexico
Growth Difficulty: 1/3 **Type:** Summer **Watering:** In spring and fall, water generously when the soil in the pot is dry. In midsummer, early spring, late fall, wait a few days after the soil dries out before watering. Water once a month in winter.

Characteristics & Tips for Cultivation They have large stigma and thick spines make them a strong and sharp family. The spines can be straight or curved, and can also be red, yellow, golden, or gray in color. The key is to grow them nicely is to expose them to strong sunlight and to keep them well-ventilated. They are full of nectar so they are often damaged by insects or pests. Regular repotting is necessary.

Ferocactus gracilis var. coloratus

The key to cultivating this plant is to ensure it retains its sharp, shiny spines. Expose it to plenty of sunlight and take measures against high humidity.

`Summer` `6 cm`

Opuntia
Cactaceae Genus

Place of Origin: USA, Mexico, South America **Growth Difficulty:** 3/3 **Type:** Summer **Watering:** In spring and fall, water generously when the soil in the pot is dry. In midsummer, early spring, late fall, wait a few days after the soil dries out before watering. Water once a month in winter.

Characteristics Opuntia have fan-shaped or spherical stems that grow in piles. They are highly adaptable to their environment, tough, and easy to grow. The two varieties listed here are popular varieties also known as "Uchiwa Cactus" and "Bunny Ears." They are densely covered with fine inverted spines, which are difficult to remove and painful when they get stuck, so be careful when handling them.

Opuntia microdasys *'Uchiwa Cactus'*

`Summer` `7 cm`

Opuntia microdasys var. albispina *'Bunny Ears'*

`Summer` `7 cm`

Cintia
Cactaceae Genus

Place of Origin: Bolivia **Growth Difficulty:** 1/3
Type: Spring-Fall **Watering:** In spring and fall, water generously when the soil in the pot is completely dry. Stop watering during summer and water sparingly during winter.

Cintia knizei

`Winter` `7 cm`

It has a mysterious shape that looks like a cluster of beans. This genus is a relatively new face, officially recognized in 1996. It was originally circulated under the name "Napina brocade." It's native to Bolivia's tall mountains at 9800'/3000m, with most of the plants body growing buried underground. It's weak to strong direct sunlight and high humidity. Protect it with shade nets in midsummer.

Leuchtenbergia
Cactaceae Genus

Place of Origin: Mexico **Growth Difficulty:** 3/3
Type: Summer **Watering:** From spring to fall, water generously when the soil in the pot is dry. As temperatures fall, gradually reduce watering, and stop almost entirely in winter.

Leuchtenbergia principis

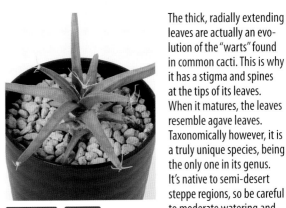

`Summer` `9 cm`

The thick, radially extending leaves are actually an evolution of the "warts" found in common cacti. This is why it has a stigma and spines at the tips of its leaves. When it matures, the leaves resemble agave leaves. Taxonomically however, it is a truly unique species, being the only one in its genus. It's native to semi-desert steppe regions, so be careful to moderate watering and ventilation to avoid high humidity and moisture.

Glossary

Aerial root Roots that grow above ground instead of underground. In the case of succulents, pots being full of roots may cause the roots to grow aerially. In such cases, the plant needs to be repotted.

APG classification system A new classification system for angiosperms as an alternative to the conventional neo-Engler and Cronquist systems. It was first published in 1998. Since then, it has been revised a few times, and the latest version is APG IV (4th edition) published in 2016. The name is an acronym for Angiosperm Phylogeny Group.

Areole The cottony part at the base of a cactus's spines. Some species have areoles despite not having spines too.

Bloom A substance found on the surface of fruit and vegetable peels and on the leaves and stems of succulent plants that looks like a white powder. It specifically refers to a wax in the cuticular layer that covers the surface of the plant body. It prevents the entry of microorganisms and the evaporation or penetration of water.

Blown offspring Refers to when side shoots or runners emerge from the parent plant.

Bract *See*: Flower bracts

Brocade (Nishiki) Spotted varieties sometimes have the word "nishiki" added to the back of the variety name.

Bulb An organ located underground in perennial plants which acts as a storage for nutrients, helping protect the plants during their dormancy. Bulbs are divided in four categories: corms, tubers, tuberous roots, rhizomes.

Central speckles Refers to a loss of pigment in the center of leaves. Depending on the color of the speckles, they can be called "white speckles" or "yellow speckles." *See*: Mottled / Speckled

Child plant / offspring shoots / cotyledon A shoot that emerges from the base of the parent plant and already has roots.

Cluster growth As the parent plant grows plenty of offspring, growing in clusters refers to multiple individual plants densely growing near each other.

Caudex A generic common name for a type of succulent with a characteristic form of clumping stems and roots. Classically, it belongs to a number of genera, including Oleaceae, Asteraceae, and Lamiaceae.

Coming to life / Taking root Refers to the process by which a transplanted plant starts to root, absorb water, and begin to grow.

Crestation / Cresting *See* : Fasciation

Crossbreeding It refers to pollination or fertilization using different species or varieties rather than the same species.

Crossed opposite growth / Crossed paired growth A type of growth in which leaves emerge from the stem at a 90-degree angle at each node, giving the appearance of cross-shaped leaves when viewed from above. *See*: Alternate Growth

Culture medium soil A mixture of several types of soil, making it optimal for the cultivation of the plant.

Cutting and planting A method of breeding plants in which branches, stems, etc. cut from the parent plant are inserted into the soil to produce new roots and shoots.

Cutting back Trimming and shortening branches or stems that have been stretching. This allows healthy branches and stems to emerge again.

Deformed leaf A leaf which has been altered so that it performs a function different from that of a normal leaf. They include bracts, nutrient storage leaves, leaf needles, insect-catching leaves, and tendrils.

Distributional name / Common name In addition to the scientific or Japanese names of plants, popular varieties or varieties with a distinct appearance sometimes have a nickname under which they are distributed and sold.

Dogiri It refers to the act of cutting the cylindrical body part of the cactus. It is a method used to re-tailor plants that have grown in bad shapes. *See* p. 58.

Dormant Period / Dormancy Both succulents and cacti have periods of vigorous growth (growth period) and periods of arrested growth (dormant period). Species native to regions that have separate dry and rainy seasons usually go dormant during the dry season. Many species drop their leaves during dormancy.

Epiphyte plants, epiphytic A plant that grows on other trees or rocks and grows by rooting on their surfaces, instead of growing on the ground. Examples include Lipsalis of the Cactaceae genus and Tillandsia of the Bromeliaceae genus. They are not parasitic but symbiotic instead, as they share their nutrients with the plant on which they root.

Fasciation A phenomenon that occurs in some plants. It refers to a mutation of the growing point (or points) in a plant and cause it to grow in an unusual shape. Succulent plants are prone to fasciation which can be classified as "petrifaction" (monstrosa), in which the growing point grows in a cluster or band, or "crestation" (crestata), in which the growing points repeatedly separate. *See*: p.47

Flower bracts Bracts are deformed leaves (p.168) that protect the flower buds. The large, petal-like bracts in some varieties are also ornamental. The Tillandsia genus in the Bromeliaceae family has brightly colored bracts which are called "flower bracts" instead.

Flower bud A bud on a stem or branch that holds an inflorescence which grows into a flower. Flower buds are generally thicker and rounder than leaf buds.

Flower stalk A leafless stem that emerges directly from the underground stem and only grows flowers. Dandelions are a common example.

Flower stalks The dead petals and stamens that remain after a flower has finished blooming.

Flower stem A stem branching off from the plant's regular stems to form a stalk that grows a single flower. A stem that grows multiple flowers is called a peduncle.

Groundcover A plant used to cover the ground surface in mixed arrangements to maintain aesthetics; prevents the soil from drying out.

Ground planting Planting directly in the ground in a garden, flower bed, field, etc.

Growing season Refers to the period when succulent plants in which they leave dormancy, sprout new shoots, and then rapidly grow new stems and leaves, also blooming flowers.

Growth type The three growth types are summer type, spring-fall type, and winter type; based on the season in which succulent plants grow most actively in relation to climate.

Half-shade A location outdoors in bright sunlight but not in direct sunlight, such as under the eaves of a roof. Alternatively, a location where the plant is exposed to the sun only for a few hours a day or shaded by a shade net. *See* p.21

Herbaceous plants Also referred to as herbs. Depending on their growth period, they are classified into annual, biennial, and perennial herbs. Annual and biennial herbs flower, fruit, and die within one or two years, leaving seeds. Perennials are perennial grasses that sprout in spring even after their above-ground parts die back in winter. Opposite to woody plants

Hybrid species / Hybrids The result of crossbreeding between two genetically different individual plants. Cross breeding can happen either intentionally (horticulturally) or accidentally in nature.

Imported plants Succulents and cacti collected as they were growing in their native regions and imported.

Inflorescence Indicates the flowering stem in general and its arrangement style. Examples: racemes, acicular inflorescences, etc.

Irrigation Watering plants.

Lawn cloth A material used to cover plants to protect them from cold, insects, and shade them from light. It's a thin cloth made of chemical fibers woven into a mesh pattern.

Leaf burns / Leaf scorches A condition in which the surface temperature of leaves rises rapidly due to exposure to strong sunlight, resulting in cells getting scorched and dying. *See:* p.37

Leaf insertion A method of growing new offspring peculiar to succulent plants in which a single leaf is used to germinate and root the plant and allow it to grow.

Leaf watering Watering the leaves lightly, just enough to wet them. This should be done occasionally for few varieties that absorb morning and evening dew on their leaves. This method can also be used to lower the temperature of the plant. After watering leaves, dry the off the remaining water thoroughly in a well-ventilated place.

Lignification Lignin accumulates in the cell walls and hardens them, turning them into wood. Lignin is a high-molecular compound that is an essential component in wood.

Lower leaves Leaves growing on the lower part of a stem.

Mixed arrangement An arrangement of multiple varieties in a single pot or container.

Monstrosa *See:* Fasciation

Native habitats Habitats where the plants can indefinitely reproduce on their own. Unlike the "place of origin," which refers to where a species first appeared, native habitats include regions where the plant have also been spread to.

Node interval / Internodes The parts where leaves and branches emerge are called nodes and the spaces between them are called node intervals. The length of node intervals varies depending on the environment in which the plant is grown. For example, if the plants lack sunlight, node intervals grow longer than normal.

Opposite growth A type of leaf and branch growth: from one single growth point, leaves or branches grow two at once at a time on opposite side. *See* also: Reciprocal Growth

Original species/variety The parent or ancestor species from which improved variants or hybrids were derived: these species also still grow untouched by men in the wild.

Ornamental border A type of speckles that grow around the edges of the leaves.

Ouhi Species that contain the word "ouhi" (or "queen") in their scientific name or Japanese nickname, are usually smaller variants. Examples: Crassula 'Ouhijintou', Agave Potatorum 'Ouhi Raijin.'

Outdoor cultivation Refers to a type of cultivation in which plants are grown outdoors in a nature-like environment, without the use of special facilities such as greenhouses or heated beds.

Parent stock / Parent plant The original stock from which the plant is bred and planted or divided.

Petal Generally refers to the petals of flowers.

Petrification. *See*: fasciation

Phyllotaxis Refers to the phenomenon in which the leaves of a plant are arrange with a specific regularity around the stem. Alternate, opposite growth etc.

Place of origin The original habitat or place of origin of plants and animals.

Plant separation/division A method of increasing the number of plants by dividing the offspring from the parent plant. As the offspring already have roots, there is little to no chance of failure.

Planting buds Offspring branches, stems, or leaves separated from the parent plant and used for planting.

Propagule The part of an axillary bud (a bud that emerges from the base of a leaf) that accumulated nutrients and has grown thick. It is one of the vegetative reproductive organs of a plant. When the buds fall off the parent plant, they germinate and grow into a new plant.

Racemous inflorescence, Raceme An inflorescence in which many flowers with a floral peduncle are borne on a long, elongated inflorescence axis, as in the case of a Fuji flower.

Reciprocal Growth A type of leaf and branch growth: from one single growth point, leaves or branches grow one at a time in opposite side. *See* also: Alternate Growth

Repotting / Replanting Replanting is the process of transferring a plant to another pot or other container. The old roots are cut away and the previous soil is replaced with a new soil. It is best to do this before the growth season.

Ridge Refers to linear or angular ridges on the surface of a stem or fruit. The number of ridges that appear on a variety with ridges is usually fixed. If the number of ridges is different from usual, that is called "ridge variation" and is highly prized.

Root clogging You can determine that the pot is clogged with roots when it takes a longer time for water to drain from the pot during watering. When roots are getting clogged, the ventilation and drainage get worse, causing the plant to generally weaken. It requires repotting.

Root rot A condition that affects the roots, mainly caused by overwatering. As the roots lose the ability to absorb water, the plant will die if left unchecked.

Rosette Refers to radical leaves (leaves growing from roots) growing densely in a radial shape. The word "rosette" is derived from "rose," as the pattern resembles a rose's flower. Many plants, such as dandelions, survive the winter in a rosette status.

Rosette-like shape In genus like Echeveria and Graptoveria, the terms "rosette" or "rosette-like" are used to describe the rosette-like shapes of the plants.

Runner A stem that grows horizontally to the ground from the base of the stem. Unlike creeping branches, runners don't grow roots from the middle of their stem.

Scientific nomenclature They are generally composed of "family name + species name," with subspecies, varieties, hybrid, and other horticultural details attached to the end.
ssp. : abbreviation of subspecies
sp. : abbreviation of species
var.: abbreviation of variety
hyb.: abbreviation of hybrid
f. : abbreviation of forma

Seedling A seedling is a plant that grows from a seed germinating, instead of planting cut parts from other trees. It also refers to the action of planting and cultivating seeds from a plant.

Self-pollination or self-fertilization Refers to plants producing fruits by getting fertilized from their own pollen. Also called self-fruiting. Self-pollinating species tend to grow fruits even if there is only one plant, but

Serrations Refers to the jagged shapes on the edges of leaves. The tips of the serrations usually point toward the tips of the leaves.

Shade net Nets used exclusively to protect plants from direct sunlight and high temperatures. There are a variety of colors and percentages of sunlight blockage to choose from, depending on the intended use. When used for succulent plants, a net with a shading ratio of about 50% is suitable.

Shading The act of blocking direct sunlight with a shade net or cloth.

Shrub A woody plant less than 1–10' (0.3–3m) tall. Usually, the main trunk and branches are not distinctly separated and some branches grow directly from the roots. Trees over 10'/3m in height are called tall trees.

Slow-releasing fertilizer A type of solid fertilizer which contain chemicals that dissolve over time for a long-lasting effect.

Speckles A dotted pattern.

Spike (inflorescence) A type of inflorescence with many small flowers on a long axis. Similar to a raceme, but the individual florets are not attached to the petiole.

Spine / Spike / Thorn A general term used to refer to the pointed tips protruding from the surface of a plant's body. Depending on their shape, they are categorized as "strong spine," "straight spine," "curved spine," or "hooked spine."

Spring-Fall type *See*: p.24

Stem The part of the plant above the ground that holds up the plant and grows leaves. The vascular bundles, which provide passage for water and photosynthetic products, are developed in the stem. *See*: Trunk (p.168)

Stipule One of the organs that make up a leaf, can grow in many shapes (leaf, protuberance, spine). Its function is to wrap and protect the buds.

Stretching A condition in plants caused by lack of sunlight in which stems and branches stretch and become thinner than is usual.

Succulent plant A general term for plants whose leaves, stems, or roots have "succulentified," which means they have grown(evolved) to being filled with water and nutrients. The term succulent is not a botanical taxonomic classification, but a horticultural one.

Summer type *See*: p.24

Tailoring Tailoring is the process of growing and shaping a tree or bonsai. This is done by shaping the trunk, branches, leaves, and such into the desired form. In a broader sense, it also includes all sorts of maintenance work.

Trichome Refers to the fine hairs on stems, leaves or flowers. They have various functions depending on the species: protecting the plant from strong sunlight; preventing excessive loss of water from the skin surface; protection against small insects and pests.

Trunk A stem in which the fibrovascular bundle has turned wood-like. Strong and hardened perennial stems are called tree stems; thickened tree stems are called trunk. *See*: Stem

Trunk standing / Standing on its trunk / Growing upward A way to define a type of growth in succulents. It indicates that the plant is growing upward in a vertical direction. Can also be called "stem standing" or "tree standing."

Tuber A tuber is an underground stem that has grown into a thick engorged mass. Anemones and cyclamen have tubers. In some succulent genera, such as pachypodiums and adeniums, most of their species are tuberous species with enlarged stems growing either underground or over the surface.

Tuberous root The root of a plant that has enlarged to a tuberous form and is filled with nutrients.

Underground stem A stem that burrows into the ground. In the case of Haworthia and Agave, new branches grow out of the underground stem, and the offspring emerge. Some grow fat with water and nutrients and become tubers.

Variegated /spotted A variation of pigmentation that's usually caused by a genetic mutation. The natural pigment present in the plant is missing and some green parts of the plant appear white or yellow.

Variety / Species Strictly speaking, a species would be classified into a "subspecies," "variety," or "variant," but for simplicity in this book I refer to most plants as varieties.

Verticillation When multiple leaves grow from each stem node. When the number of leaves on each node is fixed, they can be called three-ringed or four-ringed varieties.

Washington Convention CITES Officially known as the "Convention on International Trade in Endangered Species of Wild Fauna and Flora." This treaty was adopted in Washington, D.C., in 1973, and is commonly referred to as the Washington Convention. In order to prevent the extinction of species due to excessive international trade for commercial purposes, CITES lists species of wild animals and plants that are considered to be in need of protection in the Appendices, and regulates international trade by dividing the contents of the Appendices into three categories according to the degree of threat of extinction. International trade for commercial purposes is prohibited in principle for species registered in Appendix I.

Water cutoff When succulents and cacti go into dormancy, watering should be reduced as much as possible. Some succulents and cacti can have their watering completely cut off during their dormancy, while others, with thinner roots, need a small amount of water once a month during their dormancy too.

White powder *See*: Bloom

Window The transparent part of the leaves in Haworthia, Conophytum, Lithops, etc. In their native habitats, many species have most of the plant body submerged in the ground, leaving only the "window" at the leaf tip above the surface, and photosynthesize the light absorbed through the window.

Winter type *See*: p. 24

Woody plant Commonly simply called a tree. The part above the ground in a woody plant survives for many years, repeatedly flowering and fruiting, and growing thicker. Opposite of: herbaceous plants.

Index of Plants

"Books to Span the East and West"

Tuttle Publishing was founded in 1832 in the small New England town of Rutland, Vermont [USA]. Our core values remain as strong today as they were then—to publish best-in-class books which bring people together one page at a time. In 1948, we established a publishing outpost in Japan—and Tuttle is now a leader in publishing English-language books about the arts, languages and cultures of Asia. The world has become a much smaller place today and Asia's economic and cultural influence has grown. Yet the need for meaningful dialogue and information about this diverse region has never been greater. Over the past seven decades, Tuttle has published thousands of books on subjects ranging from martial arts and paper crafts to language learning and literature—and our talented authors, illustrators, designers and photographers have won many prestigious awards. We welcome you to explore the wealth of information available on Asia at **www.tuttlepublishing.com**.

Published by Tuttle Publishing, an imprint of Periplus Editions (HK) Ltd.

www.tuttlepublishing.com

YOKUWAKARU TANIKUSHOKUBUTSU
Copyright © NIHONBUNGEISHA 2021
supervised by Shoichi Tanabe
English translation rights arranged with
NIHONBUNGEISHA Co., Ltd. through Japan
UNI Agency, Inc., Tokyo
English Translation © 2023 by Periplus Editions
(HK) Ltd.
Translated from Japanese by HL Partners LLC

ISBN 978-0-8048-5553-2

Plant Arrangement Production
*Mika Maruyama (pp. 8–11, 38–39),
*Tanabe Flower (pp.12–16)

with Cooperation from
*Atsumi Engei, *Tsutomu Miyazaki
<PRICK GARDEN CACTUS Miyazaki>

Staff
Editing and composition: Eiko Ozawa <GARDEN>
Photography: Norihito Amano (NIHONBUNGEISHA)
Writer: Yoko Oizumi

Editorial Cooperator: Mayuko Oizumi
Illustrations: Yoko Chihara
Design: Reiko Harajo Design Office

Distributed by

North America, Latin America & Europe
Tuttle Publishing
364 Innovation Drive
North Clarendon, VT 05759–9436 U.S.A.
Tel: 1 (802) 773 8930 | Fax: 1 (802) 773 6993
info@tuttlepublishing.com
www.tuttlepublishing.com

Japan
Tuttle Publishing
Yaekari Building 3rd Floor
5–4–12 Osaki
Shinagawa-ku
Tokyo 141–0032
Tel: (81) 3 5437 0171 | Fax: (81) 3 5437 0755
sales@tuttle.co.jp
www.tuttle.co.jp

Asia Pacific
Berkeley Books Pte. Ltd.
3 Kallang Sector #04–01
Singapore 349278
Tel: (65) 6741 2178 | Fax: (65) 6741 2179
inquiries@periplus.com.sg
www.tuttlepublishing.com

26 25 24 23   10 9 8 7 6 5 4 3 2 1
Printed in China   2304EP